GET REAL, GET READY, GET GOING

MICHAEL ROSS

Fleming H. Revell
A Division of Baker Book House Co
Grand Rapids, Michigan 49516

Published by Fleming H. Revell
a division of Baker Book House Company
P.O. Box 6287, Grand Rapids, MI 49516-6287

Printed in the United States of America

Library of Congress Cataloging-in-Publication Data

Ross, Michael, 1961–
    Get real, get ready, get going / Michael Ross.
       p.   cm.
    ISBN 0-8007-5712-2 (paper)
    1. Teenagers Prayer-books and devotions—English. 2. Devotional calendars. I. Title.
    BV4850.R67   1999
    242'.63—dc21   99-33492

Scripture quotations are from the HOLY BIBLE, NEW INTERNATIONAL VERSION®. NIV®. Copyright © 1973, 1978, 1984 by International Bible Society. Used by permission of Zondervan Publishing House. All rights reserved.

The introduction "Time for Action!" on pp. 9–10 is adapted from "The Ghost of Christmas Future" by Joey O'Connor, *Breakaway* magazine, December 1995, and is reprinted with permission of Focus on the Family.

The story "Faith through the Flames" is adapted from *Breakaway* magazine, May 1997, and is reprinted with permission of Focus on the Family.

The story on pp. 41–43 is adapted from "Don't Get Burned" by Tom Neven, *Breakaway* magazine, October 1997, and is reprinted with permission of Focus on the Family.

The story "Faith against the Odds" is adapted from "Taking on a Giant" by Susie Shellenberger, *Brio*, November 1997, and is reprinted with permission of Focus on the Family.

The story on pp. 109–11 was inspired by the book *Joan 'n' the Whale* by John Duckworth, © 1987 by Fleming H. Revell.

For current information about all releases from Baker Book House, visit our web site:

http://www.bakerbooks.com

To
my mother, Ruth,
my sisters, Barbara and Kathy,
and my brothers, Jerry and Robert.
In memory of my father, Ron, and my brother, Donald.

For God so loved the world that he gave his one and only Son, that whoever believes in him shall not perish but have eternal life.

John 3:16

Contents

Time for Action!

Picture yourself surrounded by eerie tombstones on a cold, winter night. As you tiptoe past each graveside, an unrelenting wind stings your face and whisping billows of scurrying leaves scrape across the gray-flecked, granite-carved monuments.

Each tombstone marks the spot of deceased strangers—fathers, mothers, grandparents, aunts, uncles, brothers, sisters, and children. Suddenly, you recognize some familiar names on a particular group of tombstones.

"No way," you gasp. "This can't be true!" You are shocked to discover your family plot.

That's Mom and Dad's grave! And next to them is my older brother's plot. He died at the age of—GULP!—seventy-two.

Next you spot your younger sister's grave. The headstone explains that she died of cancer at thirty-three, leaving behind her husband and two small children.

What's going on here? you say to yourself as you struggle to figure out what's happening.

As you walk through your family plot, you begin to feel strange. You look down and see a brown wooden cane grasped by a worn, wrinkled hand—your hand! Just then, that creepy *X-Files* theme song kicks in.

"AAAAARRRRGGGG!"

It's a dream. That's it. I'm having a nightmare. Guess I should lay off the Surge—and stop watching Mulder and Scully.

Then you look down again. Sure enough—your wrinkled claw of a hand is gripping a cane. What's more, each step you take is a slow shuffle. Your arthritic bones ache from the chilling cold. You pause to rest. You're old. Tired. Worried. Anxious. Scared.

Not watching your step, you suddenly trip over a shovel lying next to a freshly dug grave. After almost falling into the six-foot-deep pit, you stumble onto a small pile of dirt and sod. Glancing down, you discover a new, polished tombstone staring up at you with this menacing reminder:

You're Next
1981–?

Tablets of Human Hearts

What will be carved on your tombstone? When your life is over, what will others say about you? Will your days on planet earth be tarnished with regrets—or will your life read like a letter from Christ? (See 2 Cor. 3:2–6.)

The Bible says that everybody will stand before God to give an account for his or her life. Jesus told his followers that death was not an option but an inevitable reality for every person. But he also gave the world the greatest news ever: "For God so loved the world that he gave his one and only Son, that whoever believes in him shall not perish but have eternal life" (John 3:16). He promised eternal life to all who accept his sacrificial death on the cross and live according to his design for their lives.

The fact that you're reading this book means you want to grow in your faith, figure out God's will for your life, and reach your friends with the greatest news ever.

But where do you begin?

Step 1: Get Real

When Jesus lived on earth, he encountered many religious phonies. He called them "whitewashed tombs, which look beautiful on the outside but on the inside are full of dead men's bones" (Matt. 23:27). There's one person, however, in whom you'll never find even a hint of phoniness. In the days ahead, you'll read about him and study about him. As you do so, you'll discover that Jesus Christ is genuine Christianity personified. What's more, you'll learn how to get real about getting to know him— and about sharing him with others.

Step 2: Get Ready

Don't hold back. Tell God about all the junk you want him to clean out of your life. Tell him you want to stop being a phony, lukewarm Christian—and to start being genuine like his Son. Remember this: "If we confess our sins, he is faithful and just and will forgive us our sins and purify us from all unrighteousness" (1 John 1:9). Confess your hypocrisy as often as you sense its presence. The Bible's truth never wears out.

Remember, living a genuine Christian life is not only your job; it's also Jesus Christ's. Take hold of this truth:

"I have been crucified with Christ and I no longer live, but Christ lives in me" (Gal. 2:20). The more you seek him, the more you find that he lives his life through you. Sound confusing? Don't worry. In the days ahead, he'll teach you the meaning of Galatians 2:20. And as that happens, the result will be real—not your own weak attempt at being a "good Christian." One more thing: As you learn to be real with Jesus, you'll learn the importance of being ready—ready to defend what you believe, ready to give answers to questions about your faith, ready to follow Christ anywhere he takes you.

Step 3: Get Going

By the time you're, say, seventy, what would you like your relationship with God to be like? Will you have been faithful to God? Will you have forgotten him? What will you have accomplished for God or for yourself? What will your most important relationships look like? Whom will you have significantly influenced for God's kingdom? Will the temptations, hassles, and doubts you struggled with as a teenager have brought you closer to God or pushed him away? Will others say that you fought the good fight, finished the race, and kept the faith? (see 2 Tim. 4:7).

Jesus promises to be the author and perfecter of your faith. He promises to finish what he started. He promises to guard what he has given you. He promises to never leave or forsake you. Jesus will give you a way out when you're tempted because he is faithful. When you're an old man or woman, do you want to look back on your life with a sigh of relief—or a sigh of regret? If you want to live a life with no regrets, then it's time to get going.

It's Transformation Time!

This book is designed to help you get real about God, get ready by becoming grounded in his truth, then get going.

Is this a devotional? Is it a witnessing book? Is it a small group study guide? Actually, it's all three! Inside you'll find . . .

> ▶ discussion starters called "Reality Bytes"—featuring stories about real-life teenagers
> ▶ daily devotionals called "Truth Encounters"—designed to help you discover who you are in Christ, the basics of what Christians believe, how to grow in your faith, and a plan for knowing where you're headed in life
> ▶ helpful witnessing tips called "Salt and Light"—packed with ideas for sharing your faith

Dive into this resource and read it from cover to cover for one month straight, and I guarantee you'll see a change in your spiritual life.

PART 1

KNOW WHO YOU ARE

Reality Bytes

Faith through the Flames

A mistake.

An explosion.

In the blink of an eye life is altered forever.

Brian Sakultarawattn (pronounced skool-tra-WATT) is alone in the woods—caught in a massive wall of flames. The nineteen-year-old drops to the ground and begins to roll, but the fire won't go out. Brian screams, but no one responds.

Exhausted, he closes his eyes and lies silent—waiting to die.

My life is over, he tells himself. *I trust God.*

Brian hears a voice and opens his eyes. Everything's fuzzy. The flames are gone, but he can't move his arms or legs. Worried faces stare down at him—first his friend Dan and Dan's wife, Angellee, then a frenzied crew of doctors and nurses in white masks.

Needles and IVs are jabbed into his scarred body. Across the sterile room a monitor blips irregularly. His life is teetering on the edge. *Is this a dream?* he wonders. *Will I wake up and continue with my normal life? What about Haley? Will we get married and build the log cabin we've dreamed about? Will I still be able to work?*

I trust God.

"Hang in there," a voice says. "We're taking care of you. You're going to make it."

Just before everything goes black, Brian takes a labored breath, and three words roll off his tongue: "I trust God."

Caught in the Flames

Less than an hour earlier, Brian had been cleaning the shop at Teen Trees International, a tree farm near his home in St. Helens, Oregon, where he had been working for two years, learning forestry management skills. That morning the teen and his supervisor, Dan Kloppman, Haley's brother-in-law, had dumped a few loads of discarded paper into a burn barrel in the parking lot and lit a match.

Dan and Brian broke for lunch around 12:30 P.M., letting the fire smolder in the barrel. A short time later, Brian returned and built up the fire again. Suddenly, the flames began to shoot above the barrel's rim. Brian looked around the shop for a bucket of rainwater to dowse the fire, but he grabbed a can of gasoline by mistake.

KABOOM!

A swirling fireball torched Brian's hair and clothes. Looking through the flames, all he could see was gravel. He dove to the ground anyway and began to roll frantically, but the flames wouldn't go out. He jumped to his feet and raced to a steep dirt embankment, then rolled some more. Nothing would stop the fire. Brian screamed, but no one responded.

"I just relaxed my body and waited for God to take me home," Brian says. "It sounds amazing, but at that exact moment, I don't remember feeling a thing. The pain didn't come until later—not until my body began to heal."

Hearing Brian's screams, Dan raced over and put out the flames using his hands. Then he and Angellee loaded the teen into a van for the twenty-mile drive to the hospital. "I knew it was Brian's only hope," he says. "He was too badly burned to wait for an ambulance. I feared that he might go into shock."

"You're not going to die," Angellee told Brian, holding his head.

"I knew Brian was barely holding on," Angellee said. "I knew I had to do everything I could to encourage him."

Brian looked up at her. "I trust God," he said. "If I die, tell Haley that I love her."

A Critical Decision

An hour after the accident and fifty miles away at Emanuel Hospital in Portland, Dr. Joe Pulito of the Oregon Burn Center took Brian's family into a private room.

"There's a 90 percent chance Brian will die," the doctor said. "Maybe not in the next twenty-four hours, but infection will set in during the next few weeks, and he'll eventually die."

"So there's a 10 percent chance my son will live?" asked Brian's mom.

Dr. Pulito rubbed his eyes and took a deep breath. "Perhaps even less." (Later, the physician admitted that the odds of Brian surviving were only one-tenth of 1 percent!)

"Doctor, we won't hold you responsible for the results," Brian's mom said. "Just do your best. God will decide the outcome."

Dr. Pulito nodded his head.

The crew at the burn unit had the awesome challenge of reconstructing Brian's exterior shell—the gatekeeper against lethal infections. Unlike a first-degree burn that reddens the skin, such as the kind you get when you spend too much time at the beach, third-degree burns destroy the dermis—the capillary-rich layer of skin just below the outermost skin surface. These kinds of wounds are dangerous because they leave the body defenseless against invading germs.

Despite the slim odds, the teen had youth on his side and his heart was strong. He also had a few patches of unburned skin on his lower stomach and back that could be used for grafts.

Meanwhile, Brian's parents, brothers, sister, and Haley kept a constant prayer vigil. "That night, we slept in waiting room chairs," Haley says. "And the next day, we were joined by dozens of people from the community." At one point, more than sixty people scrunched into the waiting room.

Critical Condition

During the next several days, Dr. Pulito's team was in a race against time. Using skin from cadavers and grafts from what little flesh Brian had left, surgeons stapled together an intricate quilt of skin.

The blanket of cadaver skin was merely temporary; it bought the doctors enough time to grow skin in a lab from a small graft of Brian's own skin, a process that usually takes about four weeks. Later, when Brian's new skin arrived—cut into squares the size of mini Post-it Notes—doctors repeated the grueling process of scraping off the old skin and stitching on the new.

To keep Brian alive, surgeons had to sacrifice his infected limbs. He endured nineteen surgeries—nearly one a week during his stay at the Oregon Burn Unit. After one surgery, Dr. Kramer, a physician who assisted Dr. Pulito, told Brian's family, "I really did feel the presence of God during surgery. Keep praying."

Three weeks into Brian's stay, the teen regained consciousness.

"I was wrapped in bandages," Brian said, "and didn't realize that my limbs were gone. I thought I could still feel them."

Haley broke into tears when her fiancé awoke, and everyone in the waiting room that day began praising God. But Brian was still in critical condition.

"It gave us hope when Brian regained consciousness," Haley says, "yet we knew there was a long road ahead. It wasn't until two months after the accident that doctors told us Brian would survive."

Welcome Back!

Several days passed before Brian began to ask about his hands. He knew only that he was blind. His mom took a deep breath. "You were badly burned, and in order to save your life, the doctors had to amputate your forearms."

He then asked about his legs. "I told him that part of his left leg was gone and that infection might cost him his right foot," Jani, his mom, said. Brian's response: "Why didn't the doctors just go ahead and cut off my head while they were at it?!"

That's when Jani asked her son a hard question. "Do you think we made the right decision . . . keeping you alive?"

Brian paused, then answered. "Yes. I'm glad I'm alive. God spared me and will use me."

Jani called the family from the waiting room to gather around Brian's bed. Haley, who had barely left her fiancé's side, leaned close. "I love you very much," she said.

Brian turned in the direction of her voice. "Why?" he asked, knowing that his life would never be the same.

Brian's mom spoke up. "Brian, if something like this had happened to Haley, would you still love her?"

Brian paused again, then answered, "Yes." He thought for a minute. "I guess it's gonna take longer to finish the cabin now."

A New Beginning

Nearly a year and a half after the accident, Haley (then nineteen) and Brian (then twenty) still didn't question their commitment to each other. In fact, the couple got married.

"We had a small wedding with just family and close friends," Haley says. "Brian's parents added a special room on their house. That's where Brian and I live.

"It just doesn't matter to me how Brian looks on the outside," she adds. "It's what's on the inside that makes the outside handsome. And Brian's still the same on the inside. I still see that boyish smile. I still share the dream of someday raising a family. But right now my focus is on helping him to recover."

What does Brian think? "After the accident a newspaper reporter asked, 'Wouldn't it have been better to die than to live like this?' My answer: 'Life is precious and we can't take it for granted.' I thank God every day for another chance to live. I especially thank him for Haley. We will have kids. Doctors say I can father a child.

"My advice to anyone reading this: Live each day for Jesus. Don't wait until tomorrow to get right with him. No one knows what tomorrow will be like. And no matter how hard life gets, don't give up. Just because of what happened to me, I'm not ready to check out of this world. God has plans for me—and you."

Let's Talk: Discussion Starter

A violent explosion cost Brian his sight, both arms, and one leg. He'll never again get to hike through the woods near his home—or ride his skateboard or drive his car. He'll spend a majority of his time in a wheelchair, depending upon others for simple things—like a Coke from the fridge.

Before you continue, pause for a moment, close your eyes, and try to imagine Brian's world. How would you react if a horrible accident scarred your body? Would you still value your life, or would you want to die?

Now consider this: Despite the fact that Brian's world is forever altered, his foundation—Brian's faith in God—remains unshaken. According to this young man, his commitment to Jesus Christ defines who he really is as a person.

"I don't ask God why this happened to me," he says. "I ask him, 'What's next? How do you want to use me?'"

And remember what his wife, Haley, said? "It's what's on the inside that makes the outside handsome. And Brian's still the same on the inside."

> ‣ Beauty, brains, bucks. Why do so many people in this world place such high value on these three attributes?
>
> ‣ Read Romans 12:9–16. Based on this passage, what qualities are most important to God?
>
> ‣ True or false: "When my life sails along smoothly, I feel better about myself. When problems hit,

my confidence takes a nosedive." (Explain your answer.)

▸ Why should a Christian's identity be grounded in God? (For a clue, see 1 John 3:1.)

▸ Why are you so valuable to God—regardless of how you look, how smart you are, or what you do?

Truth Encounters

Day 1: Identity

Mark of the Maker

So God created man in his own image, in the image of God he created him; male and female he created them.

Genesis 1:27

Get Real

Suzie Rapp is late for class—again.

The fourteen-year-old trembles at the thought of facing another lecture on tardiness. She dreads the other students even more—their jeers, their snickers, their piercing jabs.

I hate junior high! she tells herself.

The young athlete can still taste the chlorine from the pool as she stands solemnly in the empty school hall, mustering up enough courage to enter her first period class. Suzie takes a deep breath, combs back her wet hair, and gently eases open the door.

It's a typical day for Suzie, an Olympic-bound eighth-grade swimmer from Arlington, Virginia. Her day begins and ends in the pool: up at 4:00 A.M. for breakfast, in the pool promptly at 5:00 for a two-hour morning workout, to first period class by 8:00—but she rarely makes the tardy bell—study during lunch, doze through fifth and sixth periods, and make it back to the pool again by five o'clock.

Suzie's entire world centers on swimming. Her workouts leave her very little time for friends. But as this teen always says, "I'm an Olympian in training. Swimming is my life!"

Her hard work and determination pay off. Before entering the ninth grade, Suzie competes in a national swimming event—and captures first place. Four years later, with several more victories to her credit, she graduates from high school and heads to Stanford University on a swimming scholarship. Then it happens.

After a grueling freshman year of nonstop studying and training (which means no social life), Suzie makes the Olympic team, representing the United States in the 1984 Olympic Games held in Los Angeles.

The big day finally arrives—the single most important race of Suzie's life. The competition she spent her teen years dreaming about.

The lean brunette curls her toes over the edge of the starting block and meditates on the serene blue water below her. *I have to win this event because my life depends on it,* she tells herself. *This is the Olympics—the world is watching.*

The cameras, the coaches, the spectators, the flags flapping in the distance quickly fuse into a dreamlike blur as she fights back the butterflies and takes the plunge. Her legs kick and her arms stroke as hard as they can. Just ahead is gold—Olympic gold. Just ahead is Suzie's long-awaited identity: "Olympic champion."

So is there a happy ending to this story?

If you believe the glory of being number one is all that matters, then the answer is . . . no. But if you've learned that giving the glory to the number one source of our abilities is the right focus, then the answer is yes.

Suzie didn't capture first place during the '84 Olympic Games, but she did stand on the winner's platform and receive a silver medal for the 200-meter breaststroke.

"I used to believe that people would think I was nothing if I didn't win the gold," Suzie says, looking back. "But I eventually learned that this is not where I should put my identity because it's all temporal and could be gone tomorrow."

Suzie explains that her "Olympic high" came crashing to the ground when she injured her knee and had to undergo arthroscopic surgery. Her doctor told her she might never train for the breaststroke again. Suzie was crushed.

"It was like saying 'you can't ever swim again,' because the breaststroke is my best event," Suzie says. "It hit me really hard and it made me think. I started asking myself questions like 'Why am I swimming?' and 'What's the meaning of life?'"

Suzie could see that swimming was more important to her than her relationship with God. She had attended church and Sunday school as a child, but she felt uncomfortable there "because I didn't know who Jesus was, if there is a God, or what he's like."

When she realized that her identity shouldn't be found in swimming or anything else but God, Suzie took the biggest plunge an athlete could ever make. She gave her heart to Jesus Christ and began striving for something that is far greater than the Olympics.

"I'm a child of God and I also swim," Suzie says. "If all of a sudden I can't swim anymore, I'm still a child of God—and that's what counts."

Get Ready

> **Exodus 20:22–26** What do these verses tell you about the value of human life?
> **Psalm 139:1–4** How does being known so intimately by God make you feel about yourself?
> **Galatians 3:26–4:7** Is your identity grounded in God?

Get Going

> **Don't lose your identity.** It's okay to express yourself through the clothes you wear or to excel at a sport or a hobby. But if you try to base your total identity on those things, you'll end up losing your identity—just as Suzie did. What's more, you'll end up bitterly disappointed.
> **Let God be God.** Ask him to tear down idols in your life—a relationship, a job, a possession . . . anything that you value more than him. Keep in mind that in the world's eyes your identity is wrapped up in what you do, how smart or athletic you are, and how you look. But in God's eyes, what matters is who you are—his child.
> **Find yourself in Christ.** Our Lord wants the very best for you. His plans for you are even better than your wildest dreams. Jesus doesn't look at you and say, "This is who you are—and who you'll always be." Instead, he says, "Just imagine who you can become!"

Day 2: Self-Worth

You're Not a Geek!

For we are God's workmanship, created in Christ Jesus to do good works, which God prepared in advance for us to do.

Ephesians 2:10

Get Real

Horrible Day 1

The torture feels worse than having twenty stakes driven into his heart. Fifteen-year-old Clint Jackson sits in a crowded school cafeteria—alone!

He stirs his mashed potatoes with a fork, takes a swig of milk, then looks around the room. All he sees is a sea of unfamiliar faces. And that annoying knot in the pit of his stomach tells him every face is staring at him.

I hate being the new kid on campus, he tells himself. *I hate moving from town to town. And I hate meeting new people. Why is my dad so crazy about climbing the corporate ladder? Why did we have to come to this stupid town?*

It seems as if everyone around him fits into some kind of clique: The jocks and cheerleaders sit at one table, the skateboarders and metal heads claim another, while the science and computer kids try to lay low in one corner of the room.

And me? I'm just part of the middle mass of nothingness that blends into the tabletops.

Horrible Day 2

Kelli Jones makes it to first period English class seconds before the teacher shuts the door. She flashes a grin at a friend, then takes her seat at the last desk of the last row. On the outside Kelli looks like a typical teen. But inside is another story.

I feel like I'm in a dark, cold prison cell, she writes in her journal during class. *It's really scary because the walls are closing in and there's no way out. I gained two more pounds yesterday, forcing me to wear baggy pants and T-shirts. My best friend was asked out by the cutest boy in school. What guy would want me? Everything's falling apart and I feel so lonely.*

Kelli scribbles one last line in her journal: *Something's got to change. I can't go on like this any longer.*

When I was a teenager, I didn't feel as if I fit in either. I was an artist in a school filled with jocks. While I dreamed about creating my first masterpiece, it seemed as if everyone else cared only about scoring at the next party. While I was excited about my future and all the possibilities God had set before me, all the other teens put on cynical acts, making everyone think that nothing but the moment really mattered.

Here's the crazy thing: I began to think that something was wrong with *me*. Before long, I became convinced that if you picked up a Webster's dictionary and looked up the word *geek*, you'd find my name somewhere in the definition. I imagined the definition went something like this:

geek (gēk) n **1.** an alien-like kid, usually a teenager and almost always a Christian. 2. one who drools profusely; one who picks his/her nose; one who is infected with an unusually large number of eye goobers. **3.** Michael Ross. Anyone who looks, talks, thinks, or acts like Michael Ross. *Editor's Note:* The words *geek* and *Michael Ross* can be used interchangeably and mean exactly the same thing.

As I grew older, I discovered that the geeks are the ones who stay focused on the moment, the guys and girls who don't give a rip about anything except "looking out for number one"—themselves. I learned that in reality my life—your life—is priceless. You are a valuable masterpiece, an incredible, unique work of art created by God for a purpose much greater than parties and popularity.

Get Ready

- ▸ **Psalm 139:13–16** Based on this passage, how should you view your life?
- ▸ **1 John 4:9–12** What does Christ's love for you say about your self-worth?
- ▸ **Romans 8:28–39** If God is for you, what causes you to doubt yourself?

Get Going

▸ **See yourself through God's eyes.** Genesis 1:26 states that we were made in his image and likeness. You need to understand that as you submit your life to God, you can enjoy his blessings according to Deuteronomy 28:1–14. (Crack open your Bible right now and check out these verses.)

▸ **Remind your brain (and bod) of four awesome truths:** (1) You were created by God Almighty, the God of the universe, and if God is for you, who can be against you? (2) You can do all things through Christ who gives you strength. (3) You have the potential to be at the head of the class—not the geek in the back row. (4) You can be a leader not just a follower.

▸ **Begin to talk positively about yourself.** Proverbs 15:4 says, "The tongue that brings healing is a tree of life, but a deceitful tongue crushes the spirit." From now on, replace "I don't know how" with "Now is the time for me to learn." Replace "I can't" with "I will."

▸ **Beware of the company you keep.** Proverbs 13:20 says, "He who walks with the wise grows wise, but a companion of fools suffers harm." In other words, a friend of winners will be a winner, but a friend of fools will be a fool. Now check out 1 Corinthians 15:33–34: "Do not be misled: 'Bad company corrupts good character.' Come back to your senses as you ought, and stop sinning; for there are some who are ignorant of God—I say this to your shame."

Day 3: Sinful Nature

Flawed by Sin

For all have sinned and fall short of the glory of God.

Romans 3:23

Get Real

Broken. Lonely. Desperate.

The outcast spends his life on the fringes, and his days are lived in the shadows. But news travels quickly throughout Galilee—even on these forgotten back roads.

The man knows he doesn't have a minute to waste. This is his only hope. He must reach the center of town. Not making it there means destruction, the eternal end to an already pitiful life.

The man covers his hideous physique in a smelly wrap and steps out of a dark alley. Suddenly, a scream. The man peeks out from under his hood and watches as a woman grabs her child and races to the other side of the street.

"Don't come around here!" yells a person on his right.

"Stay away!" screams another. "You know you're not welcome!"

"Get away from us, you unclean man . . . you *leper.*"

Everywhere he goes, the man faces rejection. But that doesn't stop him. He ignores the painful words and continues to hobble along the hot, dusty road—eventually reaching a crowd at the end of the way.

Standing among the people is the only man who won't reject him, a man who has the power to make him well. Right there in the middle of the crowd is the most famous person on earth. A Nazarene. A carpenter. God in the flesh. Right there—speaking to the broken, the lonely, the desperate—is a man named Jesus.

And when the leper reaches Jesus, a most incredible thing happens. The leper falls on his knees and begs, "If you are willing, you can make me clean."

Filled with compassion, Jesus reaches out his hand and touches the man. "I am willing," Jesus says. "Be clean!" And immediately the leprosy leaves the man, and the man is cured.

Amazing story. To me, it's one of the greatest accounts in the Bible.

Okay, I know what you're thinking: *Nice story and all, but the Bible is filled with way better events—like Jesus walking on water or raising a man from the dead . . . Moses parting the Red Sea . . . Jonah being swallowed by a whale, then spit out because he tasted terrible and needed salt. So what's the big deal about this scene?*

Let me explain.

You see, the leper wasn't just some no-name person who got a second chance at life. This outcast represents you and me. His repulsive, deadly disease symbolizes a malady that plagues us all. Oh, sure, we may not have a scarred outer appearance, but we are scarred on the inside. We all have a condition inside that's even worse than leprosy—or AIDS. It's eternally deadly and can kill both the body and the soul. It's a condition called sin.

When the Great Physician reached out his hand and said, "I am willing," he was talking to you and me.

When that pitiful, struggling shell of a man—that leper . . . you and me—made his way to see the Holy One and said, "You can make me clean," how did Jesus respond? Christ wasn't grossed out. He didn't spit on the man and order him to get lost. He didn't turn away his face and gag. Jesus did what only our Savior would do.

Even though we are all flawed by a sinful nature, we can be forgiven by Jesus Christ. Our lives won't come to a miserable end in the shadowed back roads of this mixed-up world. We don't have to spend our days on the fringes. If we seek out the Savior and ask to be healed, he is willing and able and faithful.

He will lead us along a new road—an eternal journey that's filled with hope, contentment, purpose.

So what's holding you back?

Get Ready

> ▸ **Genesis 3:1–24** What is sin?
> ▸ **Romans 5:12–21** What is the "gift of God"?
> ▸ **1 Timothy 1:12–20** How has Christ shown mercy to you?

Get Going

> ▸ **Know that you're forgiven.** Our Lord stretches out his hand and says, "I am willing . . . are you?" He touches your heart and forgives your sin and says, "Be clean!" And immediately, you are cleansed and forgiven— but only if you are willing.
> ▸ **Know where you're headed.** Where is your life right now? Are you still crawling . . . and clawing . . . and

inching your way through life? Do you feel like a shell of a teen that's just wasting away? Are you facing major rejection everywhere you turn? Don't let that stop you. Jesus is right here today—stretching out his hand to you. Take it. He's offering you freedom, and forgiveness, and a whole new life with him.

▸ **Know how to live.** God is concerned about every part of your life. He sees and knows about your struggles. He's got the hairs of your head numbered. He knows when you have a zit on your face and feel as if you don't fit in. And his heart is broken for you. That's the time when he sticks closer to you than a brother. He wants to guide you through the hard times. So when doubt or fear or your sinful nature tries to knock you off course—and when you find yourself face to face with temptation—don't waver. Instead, call out to Christ and get your focus back on him. By God's grace, you can walk this Christian walk—victoriously.

Day 4: Forgiveness

Judgment Day

As far as the east is from the west,
so far has he removed our transgressions from us.

Psalm 103:12

Get Real

The judge takes a deep breath, folds her hands, and looks José Chavez in the eyes. Suddenly, the fifteen-year-old knows he's in serious trouble.

His eleven other arrests were a piece of cake: After a short stay at Chicago's juvenile detention center, he was always released with a slap on the hand. Today is different. The court is actually talking about sending him away to a state youth jail.

The prosecuting attorney tells the judge he is a menace to society, while his public defender argues that he is really a nice kid who just made some mistakes. The teen's probation officer, on the other hand, throws up his hands and says he has given up on José. And now the boy's future is on the line.

José's mother breaks into tears as the judge bangs her gavel and confirms José's worst fear: The court orders that he be committed to the Department of Corrections.

A sharp pain stabs José's stomach, and he suddenly has trouble breathing. *It's not supposed to turn out this way,* he tells himself. *These people are messing with Krazy J—a guy who is too sly, too tough, too lucky, and too cool to actually get caught. Only amateurs are sent to the state jail.*

Vandalism. Theft. Gang violence. As the cold, steel doors of his jail cell slammed shut, José couldn't help wondering if he'd ever get another chance. *How'd things end up this way? Why was I so stupid? And what about my life? Did I blow it for good?*

José isn't just a character I dreamed up for this book. He's a real guy who joined a real Chicago gang—and ended up getting into some serious trouble. Check out his own words:

> The parties, the admiring girls, the missions against the opposition, the tall rank and respect I got when I beat up a rival gang member—gang banging seemed exciting.
>
> But there was another side to this life nobody told me about when I joined. I saw my partners shot. Some were seriously wounded, others died. It tore me up to go to the funeral of a guy I'd grown up with.
>
> Then there were my buddies who were sent away to prison for nearly their entire lives—twenty, thirty, forty, or more years. They even wanted to give one of my boys the death sentence. We're not talking fun and games now, but real tragedies with crying mothers, hurting sisters, and weeping girlfriends.
>
> And now I was a part of it.

On the surface, José's life reads like every other gang tragedy reported in the news. But look behind the headlines, get to know José . . . and guess what? You suddenly realize that your own life isn't very different from his. Like José . . .

you are guilty of breaking the law—God's law.

you will have your day in court—and will stand before the ultimate judge.

you are completely forgiven—that is, if you ask for it.

Get Ready

▸ **Acts 10:34–43** What is the "good news of peace"?

▸ **Romans 8:1–4** How are we set free through Jesus?

▸ **Ephesians 1:7** How can you be confident of your forgiveness?

Get Going

▸ **Accept God's forgiveness.** When you've blown it in some way, go to the Lord in prayer. Confess your sin, ask for forgiveness, and press ahead with the power of the Lord. Key verse—1 John 1:9: "If we confess our sins, he is faithful and just and will forgive us our sins and purify us from all unrighteousness."

▸ **Learn from your mistakes.** It's every Christian's responsibility to practice avoiding the traps that cause him or her to stumble. Key verse—Proverbs 26:11: "As a dog returns to its vomit, so a fool repeats his folly."

▸ **Look to the future.** Keep in mind that God isn't finished with you; the paint's still wet and your faith's still under construction. Growing up in the Lord is a lifetime process. Key verse—Philippians 3:12: "Not that I have already obtained all this, or have already been made perfect, but I press on to take hold of that for which Christ Jesus took hold of me."

Day 5: Holiness

Righteous Fire

Make every effort to live in peace with all men and to be holy; without holiness no one will see the Lord.

Hebrews 12:14

Get Real

Dense, black, mushroom-shaped clouds rise from a flaming landscape. Choppers and air tankers tear through smoke-filled skies, spraying bright red liquid on the inferno. A short distance away, two twin-engine aircraft drop men, women, and supplies. One by one, thirty parachutists touch down on the scene—ready for combat.

In the war against wildfires, smoke jumpers are the air attack. Cuby Valdez is a member of an elite team of forest paratroopers stationed in Redmond, Oregon.

His muscles stiffen as he glides over the rugged terrain, scouting out a safe place to land. Spread out below the hotshot smoke jumper are endless acres of breathtaking wilderness: lush forests, a winding stream, and rocky canyons. But less than a mile away, a giant fiery beast is closing in—destroying everything in its path. Cuby and his crew have been called in to stop it.

The suits these smoke jumpers wear are their most important piece of equipment. Without their white jumpsuits—made of lightweight, fire-retardant materials that protect them from the flames and reflect the heat away from their bodies—they'd never be able to get past the first blast of heat. Each man and woman must be completely covered or he or she can be badly burned—even killed. Some firefighters have suffered severe burns on the barest sliver of flesh exposed because of a carelessly applied glove or an improperly sealed boot.

The danger on the front lines can make even the toughest smoke jumper shake in his boots: Large fires generate one-thousand-degree heat, hurricane-force winds, and thick, black plumes of smoke that choke away oxygen and sting the eyes.

As Cuby's feet hit the ground, his thoughts focus on a verse he has taped to one side of his helmet: "Be strong and courageous. Do not be terrified; do not be discouraged, for the LORD your God will be with you wherever you go" (Josh. 1:9).

The bravery of Cuby and his crew is without question. But there's also an important theological truth hidden in their need for protection against the fiery inferno.

How many times have you heard someone claim that he'll make it to heaven because, while he might sin a little, he's really no worse than anyone else? He's got it all wrong. God doesn't grade on a curve. No amount of "good" deeds will tip the scale in a person's favor on judgment day. Jesus tells us, "Be perfect, therefore, as your heavenly Father is perfect" (Matt. 5:48). The standard is not "good enough"; it's *perfection!*

"Whoa," you say. "*Perfection?* That's impossible! If I have to be perfect, then I don't stand a chance."

Even a single sin—looking at someone with impure thoughts or disobeying your parents—is like a crack of exposed skin in a firefighter's suit; it'll kill you.

That's because God is holy. He can't help but be that way. It's part of his essence, his nature. His holiness is difficult to comprehend because, as sinners, we are so far from it. And as fire can't help but burn every unprotected thing it touches, God's holiness cannot help but destroy every unholy thing that comes into his presence.

But you *do* have something to protect you from God's holiness. As the firefighters are made fireproof by their suits, you can be made "holy-proof." Your suit is Jesus Christ himself. The apostle Paul writes, "You are all sons of God through faith in Christ Jesus, for all of you who were baptized into Christ have clothed yourselves with Christ" (Gal. 3:26–27). Christ wraps us in his holiness, and when we come into God's presence we are protected. There are no gaps in this suit. It's as if Jesus "took off the suit" and exposed himself to the fiery heat of God's holiness and justice to take the punishment for us. Now *that's* incredible love!

Get Ready

- ▸ **1 Samuel 6:20** How can a sinner stand in the presence of a holy God?
- ▸ **Isaiah 6:5** What gives you the confidence to stand before the Lord on judgment day?
- ▸ **2 Corinthians 5:21** Are you "the righteousness of God"?

Get Going

▸ **Don't try to earn your way into heaven.** It just can't be done. Nothing you do, including "good" works, can protect you from the burning flame of God's holiness. Imagine putting on your rattiest clothes to go fight a fire. That's kind of what Isaiah had in mind when he wrote, "All our righteous acts are like filthy rags; we all shrivel up like a leaf, and like the wind our sins sweep us away" (Isa. 64:6).

▶ **Trust Christ and what he accomplished by his death and resurrection.** The firefighters have intellectual knowledge that their suits will protect them, but it takes faith and trust to step into the flames while wearing them. That's what you have to do. You can intellectually know everything there is to know about the Bible, but until you put all your trust in what it says, it's just that—head knowledge. Until you put on the "suit" and step out in faith, you're not protected.

Day 6: Servanthood

Be a Barrier Buster

The King will reply, "I tell you the truth, whatever you did for one of the least of these brothers of mine, you did for me."

Matthew 25:40

Get Real

It's an incredible sight!

Stretched out before Nehemiah, all along Jerusalem's broken walls, are hundreds of men. Half of the busy crew is working tirelessly day and night, rebuilding the crumbled structures, while other men—equipped with spears, bows, shields, and armor—watch and wait for the enemy.

Nehemiah and his workers have confronted what looks like an impossible challenge: rebuilding Jerusalem's toppled walls in the face of fierce opposition.

Striking a balance between prayer and action, this hero of the faith doesn't give up. He has armed the workers with weapons, positioned armies all around Jerusalem, and commanded his Jewish brothers and sisters to persevere with the hope of God in their hearts.

In the process, Nehemiah has lifted the spirits of a despondent people and has restored their faith—just as he is restoring their city. His actions speak loudly to all generations: The best way to resist the Lord's enemies is to get on with the Lord's work.

New York City is much different from the Jerusalem of Nehemiah's time. Yet the "walls of morality" in much of this modern metropolis are cracked and worn—bombarded by pain, despair, and sin.

In one Manhattan neighborhood—Hell's Kitchen—anything goes. And from Forty-second Street to Times Square, pimps—often decked out in gold chains, wide-brimmed hats, and five-hundred-dollar Bally shoes—preen along the streets, while their "ladies" seduce the young and the vulnerable. Eleven-year-olds weave in and out of the crowds, peddling everything from weed to heroin. "Take your pick—ludes, crack, dust. I've got your high."

Stubble-faced winos rest their heads in the gutters, while bag ladies, dressed in filthy, ill-fitting clothes, shuffle by with their earthly possessions stored away in shopping carts or tied in bundles to their backs.

The young and the old, the homeless, the runaways, the lost, and the forgotten all lead a bleak existence in the clutches of a brutal enemy—the street. But teenagers are fighting back. A number of young Christians from the urban enclaves of New York have taken Nehemiah's message to heart and are bringing light and hope to some schools and neighborhoods.

For nearly thirty years, young men and women associated with Urban Youth Alliance—a Harlem-based Christian ministry operated by high school and college students—have put their faith into action, taking the gospel to more than thirty public schools throughout the Big Apple.

Modeling Nehemiah's example, the group's leaders see to it that work and prayer go hand in hand. They "put on the full armor of God" and step out in faith, sometimes confronting tough opposition.

Many of the students face daily battles from school administration. Even though the teens have a legal right to meet on school grounds and hold Bible studies, some faculty members don't welcome them. Many parents don't want a Christian witness on campus either.

At one high school, the administration wouldn't allow the students to bring Bibles on campus or to pray. The youths didn't give up. Instead, they forged ahead and found some creative ways to get around their temporary barriers.

"We would work out the Bible studies in advance and type the Scriptures on paper," says Nancy, one club member. "We'd also sing our prayers. Eventually, we won the respect of school officials—and have managed to bring God's light to a spiritually dark place."

With a heavy dose of prayer and Christian service, these inner-city teens are holding their ground for Christ. Nehemiah would be pleased.

Get Ready

- ▶ **Matthew 25:31–46** How can you be Christ's hands and feet?
- ▶ **Matthew 28:16–20** What does Jesus mean when he says, "I am with you always"?
- ▶ **1 Peter 5:1–11** Are you willing to serve?

Get Going

▶ **Take the time to look around you.** Someone needs you. Someone at church, at school, at home. There's that seventy-four-year-old man whose wife has Alzheimer's disease . . . he needs someone to talk to. Then there's that couple with a handicapped child . . . they really could use a break. You don't have to head off on a mission trip to Panama to serve God. Do it every day in lots of little ways—such as taking the time to talk to that elderly man or volunteering to baby-sit for that couple with a handicapped child.

▸ **Be Christ's hands and feet.** From his birth to his death on a cross, Jesus' life is a shining example of humility and service. He reached out to those whom no one else wanted around. He brought love to the unloved, hope to the hopeless. How about you? Ask God to find at least one non-Christian person you can reach—through prayer, as well as service.

▸ **Get involved!** Get involved at church, at school, in your community . . . and be salt and light to the world.

Day 7: Witnessing

How Do You Smell?

For we are to God the aroma of Christ among those who are being saved and those who are perishing.

2 Corinthians 2:15

Get Real

Fifteen-year-old Brian Cowdrey pokes his head into my office. "I finished stuffing the envelopes, and I just started stacking those magazines," he says. "But if it's okay, I'd like to take my lunch break early." Brian decided to spend his day off from school helping out around the *Breakaway* offices.

I glance at my watch and muster up my best slave-driver tone. "I don't know, Cowdrey. You've got a lot of work to do, and it's not even noon. Are you hungry *again?*"

"Nope," he says. "I'm supposed to meet a kid at McDonald's. His name is Ramon. I met him in the school cafeteria last week."

Brian pauses and looks away for a second. "I think he's in trouble," he says, glancing back at me. "He doesn't have any adults to talk to—any Christian ones, that is. I was wondering if you'd—you know—maybe meet him."

"Of course, bring him by."

An hour later, Brian returns with his friend.

"Ramon," Brian says, "meet *Breakaway* editor, Michael Ross."

With my eyes still fixed on my computer, I mechanically stick out my hand. Ramon grips it. Then I look up . . . and gasp.

This isn't a junior higher! He's a . . . thug!

Ramon doesn't have a nose ring or a Grateful Dead tattoo engraved on his forehead. But he is rough looking—sorta like the type who makes "deals" behind the gym after school. And he smells like heavy cologne mixed with cigarette smoke.

"What's up?" Ramon says with a half smile, his eyes surveying my office.

Oh no, he's casing the place.

Brian grins at my reaction. "Ramon is joining me at the youth revival tomorrow night."

"No kidding," I say, studying Ramon. "So, Brian says there's a lot of stuff going on in your life. Maybe we could grab a Coke and talk about it sometime . . ."

"Maybe you could come to our Bible study tonight," Brian interrupts.

Ramon nods. Brian's smile stretches even bigger.

A short time later, after Ramon leaves my office, I ask Brian to fill me in on the details.

"What do you suppose Ramon wants from you?" I ask.

"I guess friendship," Brian says. "Maybe a way out from the people he's used to hanging out with. I really want to help him, but I'm not sure how."

Suddenly, I'm the one grinning from ear to ear. "Brian, you smell pretty good to me."

Brian sniffs his jacket, then gives me a puzzled look.

"You are 'the aroma of Christ,'" I explain. "You are his witness in Ramon's life—and that makes you smell incredible!"

Brian's concern for Ramon taught me about breaking social barriers by seeing others through Christ's eyes. For some, myself included, Ramon would be scary—a social outcast. To Brian, he was a guy who needed compassion. Brian had crawled out of his comfort zone.

Living our lives in a "holy huddle" with other Christians makes us feel safe—even comfortable. When our focus is on the huddle, we don't have to deal with scary people on the outside. But here's some amazing news: Our comfort has a very low biblical priority.

In fact, Jesus doesn't care much about our comfort. If anything, he calls us to spend time *out* of our holy huddle and to influence the world for him. Throughout the Gospels we see examples of Christ making his disciples uncomfortable by befriending all kinds of people—even outcasts. True, Jesus doesn't want us to get pulled down by the wrong crowd. Instead, he wants us to extend a helping hand and pull others up.

Let's get back to Brian and Ramon. I wish this story had a fairy-tale ending—that Ramon changed his ways and committed his life to Christ. I wish he had. Brian still sees him in the halls once in a while and consistently invites him to Bible studies and youth group. But I wonder if there are other Christians who are willing to cross barriers and get into Ramon's life now, who can share with him the love of Christ. Maybe someone could pick up where Brian and I left off. Maybe you.

Get Ready

- ▸ **2 Corinthians 2:12–3:6** What does your "letter" tell others about your life?
- ▸ **2 Timothy 4:1–8** How can you stay plugged into the truth?

▸ **1 Peter 3:8–22** Based on this passage, what should your attitude be as you witness?

Get Going

▸ **Accept the call to care.** Think about modern-day outcasts: the glassy-eyed burnout at school or the dweeb who's always picked on in the halls. Would Jesus visit these people? Would he know their names, care about them, tell them stories? He would—and you should too. How? Find an outcast around you—maybe a guy or girl like Ramon— and look for ways that you can affect his or her life.

▸ **Involve your holy huddle.** There's strength in numbers. Trying to make a difference in the life of a "Ramon" can be risky. It helps to get your Christian friends involved. Make it a team effort to influence your school for Christ. And remember: While our comfort is a low priority in the Bible, God does expect us to use our brains and avoid unnecessary risks.

▸ **Be an example.** Living a double life is a surefire way to blow your witness—especially to a non-Christian. Remember, others are watching you.

Salt and Light

Scared but Willing

What?!
Me! Walk up to a punked-out skateboarder—a total stranger—and tell him about Jesus Christ! There's no way I'm gonna do that!

Roland Wiley can't believe what his youth minister is asking him to do. After all, it's hard enough just being a Christian, let alone putting his faith (and reputation) on the line.

"Look," the youth minister says, "street evangelism can be very effective. And the choice is yours. But being a Christian doesn't mean hiding behind a label. It means having the courage to be who you are and live your faith. It means stepping out with confidence."

Faith, stepping out, courage—Roland had heard this stuff before. But in the heat of battle—such as the hostile halls at school or an arena filled with rowdy skateboarders—it's hard to tell the world that you're a Christian . . . and invite others to join you.

Two weeks later, the fifteen-year-old is standing outside an arena, along with the rest of his youth group—their knees shaking and their sweaty palms clutching Bibles.

"Go for it!" says the youth minister, nudging Roland toward a group of skateboarders. "There's a guy right there—talk to him!"

Roland's head is spinning, but his feet won't move. Then his brain flashes back to camp last summer and another scary experience: the first time he ever went rappelling.

I stood at the top of a huge rock cliff, looking down in total disbelief.

"There's no way this thin line is gonna hold my weight," I complained. "It's gonna snap, and I'm gonna die!"

I'll never forget the camp director's words: "You've got to trust that the line will hold you and carry you safely to the bottom. Take a step, and have courage."

Roland looks at the kid standing a few feet away, then takes a step toward him. Okay, Lord . . . I'm rappelling—and trusting.

"Hi," Roland says, sticking out his hand and grinning. The other teen just gives Roland a blank stare, then glances at his Bible.

"My name's Roland."

The boy finally grabs Roland's hand. "Tony . . . I'm Tony."

"What I wanted to tell you about is . . . I mean, I was wondering . . ." Tony stands there—silent, expressionless. He doesn't even blink. "I was wondering if you knew . . . J-J-Jesus. I mean, Jesus Christ?"

Tony looks down, spins a wheel on his skateboard, then shakes his head.

"No?" Roland asks. "Well, I just want to say that I'm fifteen, and I'm a Christian. And it's really cool to follow Jesus."

Roland takes a deep breath and pulls a booklet out of his Bible that explains the basics. It shows a guy racing down a road in a shiny red sports car with Jesus waiting alongside the road, waiting for a ride.

"This is kinda how it is in your life right now," Roland said. "You're in the driver's seat—all alone. Jesus is completely shut out. But that's not how he wants it."

Roland's hands tremble as he flips through the pages. But Tony stops spinning the wheel on his skateboard and even looks half interested.

"This is how it is in my life. Jesus is driving the car, and I'm the passenger. And that's great, especially when the road gets bumpy or slippery. I don't have to worry about driving off a cliff because he's in control."

Roland looks right in Tony's eyes. "Understand?"

Tony smiles and nods yes. He asks a few questions, and Roland does his best to answer them. The two really seem to hit it off.

Then Roland asks, "Would you like to pray with me and commit your life to Jesus?"

Tony smiles. "Sure."

Lord, this is unbelievable, Roland prays as the two bow their heads. *You really can use an ordinary guy like me. I don't have to be scared!*

You may not be the campus all-star, but you're definitely a champion if—like Roland—you've taken the gutsy, tough steps that help make a difference in someone's life.

▸ When people look at your life, make sure they see . . .

someone constantly dying to Jesus.
a person of integrity who dares to put his or her
    life on the line for the gospel.
a teen with a sincere heart—not a guy or girl
    hiding behind a mask.

▸ Be real with God—and others. Too many teens mistakenly believe that God doesn't want them to be honest about their lives. They think he will be upset if they tell him how they really feel. But the Bible tells us that God does not want you to be superficial—in your relationship with him, with others, or in your own life. In Psalm 51:6, David writes, "Surely you desire truth in the inner parts; you teach me wisdom in the inmost place."

Be honest about your pain, confusion, or doubt—even with people you're trying to reach with the gospel. You aren't expected to have all the answers—just a committed, searching heart.

The fact is, God desires truth and honesty at the deepest level and wants you to experience his love, forgiveness, and power in *all* areas of your life. Experiencing his love doesn't mean that all your thoughts, emotions, and behaviors will be pleasant and pure. It means that you can be *real*, feeling pain and joy, love and anger, confidence and confusion. It's this kind of honesty that will attract others to the gospel.

▶ Become a thermostat, not a thermometer. A thermometer only reflects the climate around it. If the crowd is hot, the teen is hot; if the crowd is cold, the teen is cold. A thermostat, on the other hand, is independent. It sets the temperature and has the final say in how the climate will be. This type of teenager has set his dial—and has set out to influence his surroundings.

Check Your Pulse

▶ Is your identity grounded in God—or are you more of a Sunday morning Christian?

▶ Are you happy with yourself in general? Why or why not?

▶ What steps can you take to go deeper in your faith?

▶ Think through the stuff that trips up your spiritual life, then begin asking God to remove the roadblocks.

PART 2

KNOW WHAT YOU BELIEVE

Reality Bytes

Faith against the Odds

Lights flash, television cameras zoom in, and the familiar theme song fills the studio. Out walks the queen of TV talk shows—Oprah Winfrey. Today's topic: homosexuality.

As the audience thunders with applause, seventeen-year-old Melissa Wagner swallows hard, wondering what she's gotten herself into.

Tell me what to say, God, the Chicago-area teen prays silently. *This is not my soap box. But there must be a reason why I'm here today, and if you can use me, I'm available.*

Just minutes before the show had begun, Melissa had been picked out of the audience to share her Christian perspective on homosexuality.

"Oprah professes to be a devout Christian," the producer had told the audience earlier. "Yet she does not believe that it's wrong if a person chooses to be gay. Anyone here have a problem with that?"

Melissa couldn't keep quiet. *How can Oprah profess to be a devout Christian yet not follow what God's Word says about homosexuality? I've got to speak up!*

The teen stands up and raises her hand. Then the words shoot out of her mouth: "Yeah, I'm a Christian . . . and I have a problem with that."

"Would you be willing to say that on national TV?" the producer asks.

"Yeah . . . I, uh . . . guess so."

Now the moment has arrived, and all eyes are on Melissa.

"I think you're a powerful woman," Melissa tells Oprah on live TV. "Lots of people look up to you. But if you label yourself a Christian—and if you say you're going to uphold Christian values and profess all that Christianity stands for—but also say you support the homosexual lifestyle, you're contradicting yourself."

Oprah tells Melissa that she believes only *parts* of the Bible—not the entire book. "The God I serve doesn't care if you're tall, short, black, white, fat, skinny, gay, or lesbian," Oprah says. "He loves everybody."

Melissa tries to speak up again, but Oprah cuts her off and turns to members of the audience who support homosexuality. Melissa wants to say that God *does* love everyone—that's what his death on the cross was all about. The teen wants to say that he loves *all* sinners! He *doesn't,* however, love the sin that's corrupting our lives.

"Where do you draw the line, Oprah?" Melissa finally gets to ask. "How can you decide what you will and won't accept as truth from the Bible? You can't stand there and tell all these people you're a Christian if you're going to accept things that blatantly go against the Word of God. A Christian is one who is a devoted follower of Jesus Christ and all he stands for. You can't have both, Oprah. You claim Christianity yet also support the homosexual lifestyle. You have to make a choice."

Oprah has her comeback ready. "My definition of Christianity is different from yours," she fires back. Oprah tells how she believes that Allah and Buddha and several other paths lead to heaven. Melissa doesn't buy it.

"I believe John 14:6," Melissa says. "'I am the way and the truth and the life. No one comes to the Father except through me.' That's so clear. It eliminates all false teaching."

Toward the end of the show, Melissa is crying. The camera zooms in on her standing at the mike with tears streaming down her face. "It probably sounded like one more wimpy Christian who was unable to articulate her beliefs," Melissa says later. "But the truth is, I wasn't crying because Oprah was on my case—though she continually badgered me throughout the entire show. I was crying because she simply doesn't get it. The studio audience didn't get it. Our culture doesn't get it. We're being deceived and fed a pack of lies by the father of lies himself."

Let's Talk: Discussion Starter

Even though it was tough to go up against America's talk show queen, the *real* hurt came when Melissa got home. "I'm involved in a Christian club at school. Some of the Christians in our club really gave me a hard time," she says. "They'd come up to me and say stuff like, 'How can you say homosexuality is wrong for everyone? You have the right to declare it's wrong for you—but you can't claim that for everyone else.'"

Another Christian friend approached Melissa with "What would you do if two lesbians came to our club and sat in the front row?"

"What would I do with *any* visitor who comes to our club?" Melissa asked. "I'd accept them and love them."

Another teen said, "Look, Melissa, the whole reason we're Christians is because God forgives and loves us all."

"That's exactly right," Melissa responded. "And as Christians, we are to love everyone too. But we still can't make excuses for sin. We still have to stand up against what's wrong. And the Bible clearly states that the homosexual lifestyle is wrong. Yes, God can and will forgive, but he also wants to help that person change."

▸ True or False. "Tolerance applies only to people—never to the absolute truth of the Bible." Explain your answer.

▸ When we as Christians say something is wrong because the Bible calls it sin, we're not being judgmental, we're merely repeating what the Bible says. But standing up for truth isn't always easy. Put yourself in Melissa's shoes. What are some things that you'd say to point the world back to God's truth?

▸ Name three basics of the faith that all Christians need to be grounded in, and find the Scripture passages to back them up.

▸ Read Isaiah 53:10–12. How do you know without a doubt that Jesus Christ is the Messiah and not just another cool prophet?

▸ Why does sin separate God from his creation? (Check out 1 Sam. 2:2 for a clue.)

Truth Encounters

Day 8: God

Who Can Prove God Exists?

You alone are the LORD. You made the heavens, even the highest heavens, and all their starry host, the earth and all that is on it, the seas and all that is in them. You give life to everything, and the multitudes of heaven worship you.

Nehemiah 9:6

Get Real

Vanessa takes a giant gulp of coffee and slouches at the table. She suddenly wishes she could disappear.

"So let me get this straight, Vanessa," her cousin Ashley blurts out in front of all her friends. "You're a smart, modern-kinda girl, yet you actually believe in an invisible God—not to mention all those fairy-tale Bible stories?!"

Oh great, Vanessa thinks, *a theological debate right here in the middle of the donut shop.* The uneasy sixteen-year-old squeaks out a feeble "Uh-huh" between bites of her favorite donut, then locks eyes with Ashley.

"It's like I already told you a million times," Vanessa says, wiping her mouth with a napkin. "Believing in God and knowing him personally is a heart thing, not a head thing. If your heart is hardened toward him, then none of it will make sense to you."

Vanessa glances nervously across the restaurant, praying that her pushy relative will drop the subject. She can feel her other friends staring at her.

"All right," Ashley says, "what if I tell you that Santa Claus is here right now. He's eating a jelly-filled pastry at the table next to us." The other girls laugh. Ashley sneers.

"You can't see him because he's invisible," she continues. "But he talked to me. He told me that it's a sin to eat the particular type of donut you're chomping . . . and he wants you to stop. Do you believe me?"

Vanessa rolls her eyes. "Okay . . . I've been patient with you, but now this conversation has gotten way too weird."

"Come on, answer the question," Ashley presses. "A simple yes or no."

"Umm, no," Vanessa says. "Are you happy? Will you drop the whole thing and let us eat our donuts in peace?"

Ashley smiles smugly. "Yes . . . now I can," she says. "Now that you understand why I can't believe in your God any more than you can believe in my Santa."

Vanessa notices the smirk on each of her friends' faces. They all seem to be siding with Ashley, even the girl who sometimes shows up at youth group. The teen wishes she could think of some way of proving God's existence to her skeptical cousin—but she just can't come up with the right words.

I know exactly what they're thinking, Vanessa tells herself. *"What a dweeb!"*

It's little wonder that Vanessa is frustrated. God's existence can't be proven—at least not scientifically.

For that matter, we can't prove the existence of some of God's more famous human creations: people like C. S. Lewis, George Washington, or King Tut. Photographs, dollar bills, and ancient artwork provide evidence that these humans existed—but not proof. Evidence points to fact. Proof asserts a fact irrefutably.

On the other hand, we can put a drop of blood under a microscope and, through observation, give irrefutable proof (what scientists call empirical proof) of the identity of the fluid. We can even match it to a specific human or animal. But we can't give empirical proof that God exists.

The weight of historical evidence, however, not only makes it possible to believe in God's existence, it makes it difficult not to believe.

Get Ready

> **Exodus 3:1–15** What does this passage tell you about God's character?

> **1 John 4:16** If God is love, why do you think you sometimes behave in "unlovely" ways?

> **Revelation 21:1–8** What must you do to inherit the kingdom?

Get Going

> **God is who he is.** I doubt that arm-twisting or eloquent speeches can convince a nonbelieving friend that all of creation belongs to God. (In fact, arm-twisting and eloquent speeches aren't exactly God's style.) Transforming a hardened heart is actually the work of God himself. Besides, proving his existence isn't as important as telling the world what you know of his awesome nature:

God is the sovereign Lord of Scripture who speaks to humankind through his Word, acts in his creation and in history, and involves himself in the lives of his people.

God is the Shepherd who guides (Gen. 48:15), the Lord who provides (Gen. 22:8), the Lord of peace during life's storms (Judg. 6:24), the Physician who heals the sick (Exod. 15:26), and the Banner that guides the soldier (Exod. 17:8–16).

God is the Alpha and the Omega, "the beginning and the end" (Rev. 1:8).

God is Immanuel, "God with us" (Isa. 7:14).

God is our Father (Isa. 9:6).

God is holy (1 Sam. 2:2).

God is love (1 John 4:16).

God is I AM (Exod. 3:14).

▸ **God can't be forced into a box.** While evidence of God's existence can be found in the records of all the world's civilizations—one fact remains: Humans simply cannot grasp God by proofs. He is infinitely greater than what our minds can comprehend. We must approach him with faith. Jesus said, "The time has come. . . . The kingdom of God is near. Repent and believe the good news!" (Mark 1:15). God wants us to turn away from the sins of skepticism and despair, mistrust and cynicism, complaining and worry, and begin trusting the will of the one and only God; the God who is "I AM."

▸ **God gives eternal life in Christ Jesus.** God demonstrated his love for us by sending his only Son into the world to die that we might live. In Christ, God himself suffered at the hands of men and for men—bearing the penalty for our sins and giving us eternal fellowship with him.

Day 9: Fallen Man

Broken People

These are rebellious people, deceitful children,
children unwilling to listen to the LORD's instruction.

Isaiah 30:9

Get Real

One minute I'm surfing the tube—looking for something decent on TV—and the next minute, I'm outraged. *What I'm seeing can't be real!* I tell myself. *It's gotta be staged. But why? Who gets their kicks off this stuff?*

I've stumbled upon *The Riki Lake Show.* Today's topic: "Transvestite Gay Men and Their Female Lovers."

Riki is interviewing a gay man named Charlie, who is dressed like a woman, and a woman named Sarah, who is dressed like a man. Both claim to be lovers. Suddenly, the woman pulls an engagement ring out of her jacket pocket and kneels in front of the man.

"Charlie, we've been friends for a long time," she says, "and you know how I feel about you."

The man blushes, and the audience starts cheering.

"I want to spend my life with you," Sarah tells Charlie, offering him the ring. "I want to have your children. That's why I'm asking you to marry me."

The audience roars even louder. Even Riki begins to pressure him. "So what's your answer, Charlie?" Riki says. "She obviously loves you. Are you going to say no to this beautiful lady?"

"But I'm gay," Charlie responds.

"I don't care," his lover responds. "I think we can have a good life together."

After a long pause—the audience still cheering—Charlie looks at Riki and says, "Yes—I'll marry her. But only because I love that gorgeous ring!"

Twisted hearts, messed up values, complete moral disorder. That's what sin is—unfaith, unlove, unlife. It's an offense against the God of order, beauty, and justice. And you don't have to go very far to see it in living color. (Just turn on your TV.)

Unfortunately, though, it isn't just nonbelievers whose hearts can be twisted. Some who claim to be Christians—some who say they're walking in the light—still have one foot in the darkness. Some lead a double life and could easily be the next guest on Riki's show.

Case in point: A colleague at Focus on the Family asked me to pray for a man he was counseling. "The gentleman is a youth pastor," my friend explained. "He's married with a child. On the surface, his life looks picture perfect. But this guy is hiding something—a dark secret. A sin he hasn't yet confessed to his wife or his church. By day, he appears to be a dynamic man of God. But by night, he's a male prostitute."

This whole sad ordeal does have an amazing ending: The youth pastor confessed everything to his church and stepped down from ministry. More importantly, he repented of his sins and mended his relationship with his wife and with Jesus. Today, he's undergoing some heavy-duty counseling.

While the stories I've shared seem pretty extreme, they actually have relevance for our lives. You see, all sin is detestable to God—from telling a "little white lie" to committing murder. Sin separates God from humans, and that creates a problem for you and me. Even as Christians, you and I struggle with sin—and will for the rest of our lives on earth. (The only sinless person is Jesus Christ—God in the flesh.)

So what's the answer? How can sinful men and women have eternal peace with our holy God? Keep reading.

Get Ready

- ▸ **Genesis 6:1–22** Why did God send the flood?
- ▸ **Genesis 19:1–29** Why does unchecked sin always result in destruction?
- ▸ **Proverbs 14:11–14** How can you keep your life on the right path?

Get Going

▸ **Accept God's grace—his free gift of forgiveness.** God couldn't just wipe away our sins without a sacrificial death. Someone had to die for us, and the only death God could accept on our behalf was the death of his sinless Son Jesus.

> For Christ died for sins once for all, the righteous for the unrighteous, to bring you to God.
>
> 1 Peter 3:18

> For God so loved the world that he gave his one and only Son, that whoever believes in him shall not perish but have eternal life.
>
> John 3:16

Through Jesus Christ, your sins have been completely forgiven. Your slate is clean. You have a spotless record with God and can have eternal fellowship with him.

▸ **Destroy your "license to sin."** While your sins are forgiven, God does want something from you: commitment and obedience to Jesus Christ. But as you've probably discovered, that's not always easy. Your stubborn sinful nature, not to mention the sinister tactics of the evil one, sometimes prevents you from obeying God's will. But God did not leave you as an orphan.

In times of distress . . .

call out to God and he will give you the power of the Holy Spirit. "Again Jesus said, 'Peace be with you! As the Father has sent me, I am sending you.' And with that he breathed on them and said, 'Receive the Holy Spirit'" (John 20:21–22).

cling to the truth that we can handle whatever it is that God expects of us. "This is love for God: to obey his commands. And his commands are not burdensome, for everyone born of God overcomes the world" (1 John 5:3–4).

Day 10: Jesus Christ

Is He the Messiah?

And being found in appearance as a man,
he humbled himself
and became obedient to death—even death on a cross!

Philippians 2:8

Get Real

"Who is this man?"

"The real question is, who does *he* think he is?"

The teachers of the law had heard that Jesus was in town, stirring up the crowds with his radical ideas. A few of the skeptical religious leaders (known as the Pharisees) had to hear it for themselves—so they made their way into a crowded building and listened with disgust.

The young Jew before them claims to be the Messiah. He even insists that he has all authority on earth, yet he wanders the land like a drifter. What's more, he's a mere carpenter's son and hangs out with society's undesirables: lepers, beggars, prostitutes, traitors, children.

Suddenly . . . CREAK! SNAP! CRASH! Wood breaks, clay falls, dust rises.

The Pharisees glare. Jesus smiles.

A paralytic is lowered from the roof and gently placed at Christ's feet.

"Son," Jesus says, "your sins are forgiven."

Why does this fellow talk like that? wonders a teacher of the law. *He's blaspheming! Who can forgive sins but God alone?*

Jesus looks at the Pharisee. "Why are you thinking these things?" he asks. "But that you may know that the Son of man has authority on earth to forgive sins—" Jesus turns to the crippled man. "I tell you, get up, take your mat, and go home."

A miracle! The crowd gasps as the paralytic stands up and walks out the door. Everyone in the room rejoices. The teachers of the law are stunned.

"Is this man truly who he claims to be?"

Jesus became nothing so we could have everything.

He wore a crown of thorns so that we might wear a crown of glory. He ate with man so we could someday dine with God. He became sin so that we might become righteousness. He cried tears on earth so we would never shed them in heaven. He walked over dusty roads so we could walk on golden streets.

He died so that we might live.

No beauty. Isaiah foretold the agonies of Christ on the cross hundreds of years before Jesus was born. He also knew something about Jesus' appearance: "He had no beauty or majesty to attract us to him, nothing in his appearance that we should desire him" (Isa. 53:2).

If he had no beauty, why were so many people attracted to him? Christ's beauty was internal. His heart emanated unlimited love. The peace in his eyes drew crowds. The joy of his smile was contagious. Jesus didn't have good looks; he didn't need them.

No popularity. The Bible also describes Jesus as one who "made himself nothing, taking the very nature of a servant, being made in human likeness" (Phil. 2:7).

Christ was born in an animal shelter in the hick town of Bethlehem and was raised in the boondocks of Galilee by an average-joe carpenter. Later in life, in spite of the many times he helped others, people forgot to thank him, asked him to shove off, and tried to make him look stupid. Those who hung around him soon left, some of them running. If anything, Jesus had a bad reputation, bad enough to get himself killed on a cross.

No sin. The Bible stamps the words "no sin" on the person of Christ three times:

- ▸ "God made him who had no sin to be sin for us, so that in him we might become the righteousness of God" (2 Cor. 5:21).
- ▸ "He committed no sin, and no deceit was found in his mouth" (1 Peter 2:22).
- ▸ "But you know that he appeared so that he might take away our sins. And in him is no sin" (1 John 3:5).

No sin. No sin. No sin. Christ had to be without sin to qualify as the perfect sacrifice for the sin of humankind—the perfect sacrifice for your sin. As God's sinless sacrifice, Jesus made it possible for you to trust him and be forgiven.

Does he have your attention? Do you trust him? Do you want to be like him?

Get Ready

> ▸ **Isaiah 53** From this passage, do you see how everything Isaiah foretold came to pass?

> ▸ **John 1:1–14** How do you become a child of God?

> ▸ **Philippians 2:1–11** Can you sum up Christ's attitude in one word?

Get Going

> ▸ **Focus on the right image—Christ's.** Think of all the times you've spent in front of a mirror: flexing those muscles, sizing up your figure, checking out those new clothes. Jesus, plain-looking Jesus, wants to free you from the trap of "looking great." Keep brushing your teeth and wearing decent clothes, but don't go overboard. Instead, concentrate on the Christ who died an ugly death so that you might enjoy his beauty. True beauty. The kind that shines from the inside out.

> ▸ **Hang out with Jesus.** My wife, Tiffany, and I have a solid relationship that's growing and deepening as each day passes. The moment I took her hand in marriage, I knew I loved her deeply. And today, not only are we still in love, but we're also best friends. I'm proud of my wife and would lay down my life for her. I know she'd do the same for me.

Know what? My marriage has also taught me an important lesson about faith: Jesus wants us to have the same kind of deep, growing relationship with him. When I spend time with my wife, our relationship grows. But if we neglect each other . . . you guessed it . . . our relationship suffers. (And if we continued on that dangerous course, it would eventually die.) It's the same with your relationship with Jesus.

▸ **Build integrity—not just popularity.** So why the nausea when the team captain forgets to give you a high five? Why the desire to have forty-three people say hi to you in the lunchroom? Don't work up a sweat trying to be cool. You don't need a reputation. Christ didn't spend any time worrying about his reputation—yet he was the greatest man who ever walked the earth.

Day 11: The Enemy

Soul Slayer

Be self-controlled and alert. Your enemy the devil prowls around like a roaring lion looking for someone to devour.

1 Peter 5:8

Get Real

Jeremy blinks as he scans the room. The sixteen-year-old can't believe his eyes: a basement packed with people his age drinking and openly doing every kind of drug imaginable.

"Don't be shy," says the party's host, a spooky older man wearing an all-black outfit. "Join the fun."

A friend from school smiles at Jeremy. "Okay, so the guy is strange," he whispers, handing Jeremy a beer, "but he throws the best parties in town."

Jeremy pops the top off the bottle and shrugs his shoulders. *It's like a wild Halloween bash,* he tells himself. *It should be good for a few laughs.*

The teen downs a few more beers, takes his first drag on a marijuana joint, and eventually gets so stoned he can barely stand up. A few hours later, he and the other party goers are ushered down a secret passageway that leads to a dark, musty room at one end of the basement.

Once inside, Jeremy is even more stunned. A painting of a red goat's head covers a wall, and a pentagram is drawn on the floor in the center of the room. Half the crowd—including Jeremy's friend—circles the pentagram and begins chanting. A couple of guys speak out and begin making requests to Satan.

Did that guy say . . . Satan?! Jeremy asks himself, his eyes widening. *Is this for real—or is it just a weird game?*

Jeremy shrugs his shoulders again. *It's gotta be a game,* he convinces himself. *After all, the devil isn't for real.*

In the months that follow, he ends up attending several more of these "wild parties." Then it happens. Jeremy awakens one night in his bed—sensing a dark presence. His heart starts playing keyboards with his rib cage, and he has trouble breathing. The teen realizes that something evil has a hold on his life. Something very real . . . and very deadly. Suddenly, his fascination with the occult isn't fun anymore. What he thought would give him a few thrills is actually out to destroy him.

Jeremy is scared.

Don't be fooled, Satan exists.

The Bible uses various names to describe him—Lucifer, Beelzebub, the devil, the serpent, the dragon, the fallen angel, the enemy—and Scripture makes it clear that he is rotten to the core. Satan and his troops are viciously attacking the kingdom of God. His target: our souls. Just ask Jeremy.

This teen learned the hard way about the spiritual battle that's raging in the world. Although his name was changed to protect his identity, his story is based on fact.

On the surface, Jeremy seemed like a model teenager. He had committed his life to Christ at an early age and was a solid member of his youth group. He was well liked at church and was often described as "a kid with his head on straight." No one knew that Jeremy was leading a double life.

The fact is, he was bored—with church, school, and life in general. He hungered for something different from what Christianity had to offer. That's when Jeremy let his defenses down and turned his back on God. He met some guys at school who were into what seemed like an innocent role-playing game—"Dungeons and Dragons"—so he started playing. He gradually progressed to more violent occult-oriented games . . . and eventually followed his new friends to their "wild parties."

Today, Jeremy is out of the occult and back on track with God. But the young man has deep emotional scars and nightmarish memories he'll carry with him for the rest of his life.

The fact is, we're all targets of the evil one. Satan is working overtime to lure us into a hostile position toward God, and he uses every kind of distraction imaginable—boredom, selfish desires, inferiority, drug abuse, doubt, fear, materialism (the list could fill up this book).

Satan's biggest ally is your flesh itself, which is the human, physical dimension of your life that instinctively wants to live independently from God. Even though you now have a new nature in Christ, the sinful world still tempts you to return to those old ways of thinking and living. (See Rom. 8:5–8 and Eph. 2:3.)

So how can you survive? The answer is basic but vital—and one you'll find repeated in this book: Have a personal, active relationship with Jesus Christ. The Lord is your ultimate ally—your ultimate defender.

Get Ready

> ▸ **Matthew 4:1–11** What was Christ's primary weapon for withstanding the devil?

▸ **1 John 3:7–10** How can we know who the children of God are?

▸ **Revelation 12:7–17** How can we overcome Satan?

Get Going

▸ **Know the enemy's tactics.** Satan knows just which buttons to push to tempt you away from dependence on Christ. He has watched your behavior over the years and knows where you are weak. That's where he attacks.

▸ **Choose your weapons.** While you can't outsmart or outmuscle the flesh or the devil on your own, you can gain victory in your daily struggle against sin. The Lord has armed every Christian with spiritual weapons packed with "divine power": (1) The sword of the spirit, the Holy Bible, and (2) prayer. Colossians 3:16 tells Christians to "let the word of Christ dwell in you richly," and Philippians 4:7 promises that "the peace of God . . . will guard your hearts and your minds in Christ Jesus."

▸ **Follow your defender.** Merely hanging out at church and "doing your Christian duty" doesn't cut it. You need to know Jesus personally. He is the greatest conqueror ever, and with his guidance, you can have victory over the devil.

Day 12: The Holy Bible

Trust the Instruments!

All Scripture is God-breathed and is useful for teaching, rebuking, correcting and training in righteousness, so that the man of God may be thoroughly equipped for every good work.

2 Timothy 3:16–17

Get Real

"It's time to rock 'n' roll, boys," Major Gary Green ("Stash") radios to his wingman.

"We gotcha, Stash," responds a pilot whose call sign is "Shooter."

The pressure hits as two F-15E Air Force fighter jets descend to five hundred feet above the earth, accelerate to 480 knots (530 mph), and skim the ragged contour of the harsh desert below.

Today's mission: Stash and Shooter must coach an Air Force trainee through some tricky low-level maneuvers.

The landscape becomes a reddish blur as Stash's twenty-eight-ton Eagle picks up speed. He navigates his craft through canyons and over hills—sometimes sideways, sometimes upside down. Just when his trainee doesn't know which way is up or down, Stash turns over the controls.

"No matter what conditions we face," Stash tells his trainee, "always trust the instruments. Understand?"

"Roger, sir," the young pilot responds.

The trainee examines the instruments, then squints out the window. The readings just don't feel right to him.

"Rocks ahead," Shooter radios to Stash. "Roll right. Unload." (Meaning: You're gonna slam into a wall! Pull up and head out of the canyon.)

After a couple of seconds of fumbling around, the trainee is still confused—and the plane continues on a collision course with a canyon wall. That's when Stash takes over. The veteran pilot aggressively rolls his Eagle on its side and spirals out of the saddleback, barely missing a jagged ridge.

When the plane is on a safe course again, Stash debriefs his student pilot. "You didn't listen to me," Stash stresses. "I'll say it again—*never* go with your feelings in the air. Always trust the instruments."

"Yes, sir," the trainee says. "It's just that—"

"No excuses," Stash barks. "The instruments will keep you on track. Now let's go in and do it again."

The trainee swallows hard. *This time, I'll do it right. This time, I'll trust the instruments.*

How many times have you listened to your feelings, instead of trusting the instruments? (Okay, I know what you're thinking: *Stupid question. I'm not a pilot in training; I'm a teenager.*)

Actually, Stash's instructions apply not only to budding pilots; they pertain to growing Christians as well. You see, the Bible is like a panel of instruments on an F-15. You can depend on it to guide you through life and keep you on track as a Christian.

All Scripture is "God-breathed" and offers solid advice for just about every situation you'll ever encounter. Through the Word, God teaches, rebukes, corrects, and trains us in righteousness.

Without the Bible, we wouldn't know (a) what God is like, (b) his plan for humans like you and me, (c) how much he loves us, (d) the right way to live on this planet, or (e) anything about what will happen to us after death.

Don't make the mistake that sends some novice pilots off course. Trust your instrument panel—God's Word.

Get Ready

> ▸ **Psalm 119:89–112** In what ways is God's Word like a lamp to our feet?

> ▸ **Acts 17:1–4** How can we use Scripture to reason with unbelievers?

> ▸ **2 Peter 1:19–21** Name one key way in which Scripture differs from other writings.

Get Going

> ▸ **Learn what wise pilots know.** You'll hear all kinds of reasons why some people favor their feelings over the Bible: "It was written too long ago to really be relevant today." "It just doesn't make any sense to me." "No one can know for sure that it's 100 percent accurate."

Despite some people's doubts, God's Word *is* timeless and absolutely, positively accurate in everything he felt was essential for us to know. While there is room for debate on irrelevant issues (like whether Judas hanged himself or stabbed himself), there are no discrepancies in the Bible's promises, commands, and warnings. And the fact is, archaeologists and researchers are constantly making new discoveries that confirm the Bible's authority.

▸ **Know how to read the instruments.** Are you intimidated by that big, thick book with no pictures? Don't be. In order to get the most out of your Bible, you need to know how it's organized. First, understand that the Bible isn't just one book. It's actually a library of sixty-six books, or booklets, bound into a single volume! Also, it's divided into two primary collections of books.

The Old Testament contains the first thirty-nine books, which teach us the basics about life and creation, God's commitment to us, prophecies of the Messiah, and why we need Christ. It explains that sin is a failure to attain the standard God has set, a perversion of our nature, a breaking of God's holy law, and rebellion against our Creator. Here's how the Old Testament is divided:

The Pentateuch (Genesis to Deuteronomy)—the foundation of the Bible; instructs us in God's laws

The history books (Joshua to Esther)—chronicle man's rebellion and God's faithfulness

The poetry books (Job to the Song of Solomon)—the wonder, the mystery, and the majesty of God unfold in these books

The major prophets (Isaiah to Daniel)—reveal the holiness of God; a foreshadowing of the Good News brought by Jesus

The minor prophets (Hosea to Malachi)—tell of devastation, idolatry, cruelty, and the coming of the Messiah

The New Testament contains the last twenty-seven books, written by ten different authors. The New Testament begins with the four Gospels and includes a record of the spread of the Good News preached by Jesus, letters to individuals and churches, and general letters that read like sermons. The last book, Revelation (or the Apocalypse), tells of the final triumph of Jesus and the judgment of all humanity.

▸ **Set a flight path.** It's vital that you have a plan for reading the Bible. There are several ways you can develop such a plan, depending on your preference. For example, to help you understand Scripture, it's a good idea to read a Bible commentary or a daily devotional—such as this book—as you study Scripture. You can always begin by reading a chapter of Scripture at a time, but remember that the issue is not how much you read but rather that you understand what you've read and apply it to your life. Also, use a Bible version that you can understand, one that isn't a chore to read.

Day 13: Absolute Truth

From Destroyer to Defender

Immediately, something like scales fell from Saul's eyes, and he could see again.

Acts 9:18

Get Real

A hush falls over the synagogue as a fiery Jew stands before the crowd. Today's speaker: a powerful Pharisee named Saul—the persecutor.

It's no secret how Saul feels about Christianity. He detests it. And everyone knows why he has come to the Roman city of Damascus.

For some time, Saul has been heard breathing out murderous threats against the radical members of the Way— the name given to Christ's disciples. Now he is leading a campaign of repression against them and is determined to bring down his iron fist on their unorthodox teachings.

Saul's eyes scan the synagogue, studying the faces of his fellow Jews and members of the law. The words unfold slowly from his lips. "This man. . . . This man they call Jesus Christ . . . he is . . ."

Yes, Saul, get on with it, another Pharisee tells himself. *Tell the crowd that he's a liar and a fraud. Tell them his followers are a bunch of lunatics who should be behind bars.*

Saul speaks passionately. "He is truly the Son of God. This Jesus, the one I thought was dead, is alive. I've seen him with my own eyes. Those Christians are right!"

Everyone gasps.

"Isn't he the man who raised havoc in Jerusalem?" a voice shouts from the crowd.

"And hasn't he come here to take them as prisoners to the chief priests?" shouts another.

Saul emphasizes the truth. "This Jesus I am proclaiming to you is the Christ," he says. "Repent of your sins. Believe in the Lord Jesus, and you will be saved."

It's a miracle in Damascus! The stern Pharisee who was once bent on blocking the Way now burns a path for the Good News of Christ. The feared persecutor who was once blinded with hate now sees with a heart focused on love.

• It's an amazing story. Saul of Tarsus had an incredible truth encounter on the road to Damascus. He stood face-to-face with the risen Christ, and his life was forever changed.

> As he neared Damascus on his journey, suddenly a light from heaven flashed around him. He fell to the ground and heard a voice say to him, "Saul, Saul, why do you persecute me?"
>
> "Who are you, Lord?" Saul asked.
>
> "I am Jesus, whom you are persecuting," he replied. "Now get up and go into the city, and you will be told what you must do."
>
> The men traveling with Saul stood there speechless; they heard the sound but did not see anyone. Saul got up from the ground, but when he opened his eyes he could see nothing. So they led him by the hand into Damascus.

Acts 9:3–8

When Saul regained his sight, he was a new man. And a short time later (Acts 13:9 to be exact), he got a new name: Paul.

Flip open your Bible and you'll discover that fourteen books in the New Testament bear Paul's name. Each tells about a radical faith that literally turned his world upside down, a faith he wasn't ashamed to boast about.

Paul learned three truths about Christianity:

1. The crucified Jesus really had risen from the dead and truly is the Savior of all.
2. The wages of sin is death, but Jesus paid that price for humankind. Therefore, salvation is gained only through a relationship with Jesus—not by following the rigid laws of the Pharisees . . . or any other worldly philosophy.
3. Christians must never be ashamed of the Good News of the gospel and must boldly spread it throughout the world—regardless of bitter opposition.

The Lord gave Paul an important assignment: Tell others about the awesome Good News of Jesus Christ. Paul learned to make his work a priority and placed it above everything: ridicule, abuse, peer pressure, embarrassment . . . even the possibility of losing friends.

So just what can we learn from Paul? How can we fuel our faith—and keep it burning? Take Paul's radical faith steps.

Get Ready

> ‣ **Matthew 7:13–14** Why do so many stay on the road that leads to destruction?
> ‣ **John 3:16–21** Why do some people fear the light?

▸ **Romans 1:16** What is revealed through the gospel?

Get Going

▸ **Radical step #1: Get your eyes off the world.** As I travel around North America speaking or getting stories for *Breakaway,* I see the same hassles hounding youth in nearly every city: Too many teens haven't "learned to discern." They have been literally brainwashed by lies from magazines, movies, TV, and peers at school. The biggest lie teens are swallowing goes something like this: "Everyone knows being a Christian isn't cool. Following God means living a dusty, boring life, void of any ounce of fun."

The fact is, being a Christian is the most exciting, most energizing, most fulfilling adventure anybody could ever hope to embark on. Following Jesus isn't a chore or a hassle. It's a privilege! Does it mean you're not gonna have any problems? Of course not. But your heavenly Father wants you to learn how to overcome hardships. In doing so, you'll begin to understand what it really means to step out as a Christian.

Decide right now to trust Jesus with your whole heart. Ask him to help you steer clear of the world's lies and to be firmly grounded in his truth.

▸ **Radical step #2: Set your sights on the truth.** Understand that following Christ is not a passing fad. It's a step-by-step, day-by-day commitment. And like any relationship, it requires your time and devotion in order for it to grow.

Make a commitment right now to spend time every day talking and listening to God. Find a quiet, private place—your room, a lonely corner in the basement, your backyard—and unload your heart to Jesus. Thank him for the cool stuff he's done in your life, pray for others, and ask for guidance.

▸ **Radical step #3: Be bold about what you believe.** God doesn't want you to hide your faith from the world. You're called to "go into all the world" with the Good News. That could mean going next door and sharing Jesus with your neighbor, or with friends at school, or even with your own family.

Let God's love shine through your life so others will come to him. Christians aren't the ones missing out on good times . . . the world is.

Day 14: Defeating Death

The Last Enemy

The sting of death is sin, and the power of sin is the
law. But thanks be to God! He gives us the victory
through our Lord Jesus Christ.

1 Corinthians 15:56–57

Get Real

The highway traffic is jammed for miles. You tilt back
your seat and moan. "If I don't get out of this sweatbox
soon, I'm gonna die!"

Your mom is too busy gritting her teeth and clenching
the steering wheel to respond.

Just ahead, you spot the problem. A twisted pile of
metal and shattered glass lies like a smashed toy in the
left lane of the packed highway.

A shiny black Porsche, once an object of pride to its
owner, sits on its side, crumpled beyond repair. A limp
body has been pulled from the wreckage and hastily
covered with a plastic sheet. Apparently not even the

trained hands of the paramedics could resuscitate the victim.

You take a deep breath, then swallow. Later, an attending officer reports that the young driver was DOA—dead on arrival.

Death claims lives all around us every day, to the point that we don't even bat an eye at the countless newspaper stories or TV reports of someone's passing. But when death strikes closer to home, as it did with the family of the accident victim, it hits hard and deep.

Chances are, you've had your own sad brush with death—a parent who passed away when you were very young, a best friend who was killed in a car crash, a teacher or pastor who quietly went to be with the Lord.

I, too, had a heart-ripping experience with death.

It was a chilly December evening. My friends and I were lounging at my house, sipping hot tea and laughing about some crazy things we'd done. Just as I neared the punch line of another crazy story, the phone rang.

"Hold that thought," I said as I picked up the receiver. My mom was on the other end of the line.

"Hey there, Mom," I yelled. "Come on, everybody, say hello to my mom. Mother, say hi to my friends!"

"Michael, stop!" she snapped. Her voice cracked. She was crying. I knew instantly she wasn't calling with the usual warm, fuzzy "mother stuff."

"It's your brother," Mom said. "He died last night."

"Died?! . . . Robert? Jerry? Don? Which one? How did it happen?"

"Your brother Don," she answered. "He just didn't wake up this morning. He died of a heart attack."

It had been more than five years since I'd seen Don, who was twenty years older than me. Yet our long separation quickly melted away. In my mind, I could still hear his deep, rumbling voice and see his curly, brown hair.

Suddenly, I felt very cold and empty inside. Every muscle seemed to tremble. One of my friends gave me a bear hug. We both broke into tears.

It took several long hikes and many afternoons of sober reflection before I could really face my brother's death. It was hard to accept. I'd never get to see him again. I'd never get to laugh with him. I'd never get to tell him about Christ's love for him—that hurt the most.

I wasn't sure if Don was a Christian when he died. At least, I'd never taken the time to share the Good News of Jesus with him. Did he accept the Lord in his last moments? Would I see him in heaven? Only God knows these things.

Unless you've had an experience like mine, the whole issue of dying is probably the farthest thing from your mind. But stop for a moment and ask yourself a few questions: If I died tomorrow, would I go to heaven? Is death the end? How will I deal with the inevitable loss of those I love so much? Will they have eternal life?

Get Ready

> ▸ **John 11:17–44** What hope do Christians have—even in the face of death?
> ▸ **Hebrews 2:10–18** What was destroyed at the cross?
> ▸ **Revelation 21:1–8** What will he who overcomes inherit?

Get Going

> ▸ **Face the facts.** None of us is immortal. It could have been you crumpled and still inside that Porsche. I could have been that brother who died of a heart attack.

The truth is, scientists will never find a cure for death. Humankind will never escape it (on our own, that is). Someday, whether by accident or illness or old age, each one of us will die. (Unless the Lord returns first!)

▸ **Know the truth.** Death stings. It's an enemy, not a friend—both of God and of man. Worst of all, death is the ultimate bad day for those who haven't accepted Christ as their Savior.

▸ **Know where you're headed.** If you're a Christian, you know that your final heartbeat won't be the mysterious end to life. And when you stand at the graveside of a Christian brother or sister, you know your loss is only temporary. That date when you and other believers meet Jesus face-to-face will be the ultimate homecoming. It will be the grand beginning to a life that never ends.

▸ **Defeat the enemy.** Sharing the Good News is the answer. God doesn't want anyone to miss out on eternal life with him. But the bottom line is this: Those who don't have a personal relationship with Jesus—those who don't repent of their sins and accept Christ in their hearts—will not spend eternal life with God. That's why it's important to share the Lord's plan of salvation with everyone. Believe me, it's an awful feeling when a loved one dies and you're not sure whether he's in heaven with Jesus.

Salt and Light

Icy Road Awakening

I'm on Interstate 40 just west of Knoxville, Tennessee. It's late, and the snow is coming down so hard I can barely see the taillights of my friend's jeep. I'm supposed to be following him to Gatlinburg, a popular mountain resort, but I'm having trouble keeping up.

In less than twenty-four hours I'll be standing in front of six thousand winter-retreating teenagers. I'm here to cohost a glitzy New Year's Eve celebration with big names like Josh McDowell and dc Talk. (That is, if I make it.)

Suddenly, my rental car hits a patch of ice and veers right, dangerously close to a drop-off. I twist the wheel into the slide, then turn left—correcting the spinout and avoiding disaster. But just as my heart rate returns to normal, I discover that I've become separated from my friend.

He's probably pulling into Gatlinburg right now, I tell myself. *I've had enough of this icy road craziness. Time to call it a night.*

I spot a Denny's sign and decide to make a detour. A quick meal, directions to a motel, a good night's sleep— my plan is set. Little do I realize, God has another purpose for my unexpected pit stop.

"You're smart for pulling in," a young waiter assures me as he slides a cup of coffee across my table. "You'd never make it tonight—the roads are bad."

I nod and stir cream into my hot drink. The waiter pauses, then sits down at my booth.

"Can I ask you a question?" he says with a serious tone.

"Uh—sure," I respond.

"I overheard you talking to another waiter," he says. "You mentioned that you're speaking at the youth event in Gatlinburg. It's a big deal every New Year's. It's always advertised on the radio."

I nod my head again, taking a sip of coffee.

"It's a Christian event," he continues, "so I assume you're a Christian."

"Yes, I am."

"Why?" he asks, looking me in the eyes. "I mean, I'm not religious—and I don't plan to be. But I've got to know something. How has being a Christian changed your life?"

Slightly shocked, slightly overjoyed, I nearly choke on my coffee. I swallow hard, then clear my throat.

"Well, uh—do you have all night?!" I say. The young man smiles and folds his arms. I take another sip of coffee and begin.

"First of all, I'm not religious either. I have a relationship—a relationship with Jesus Christ. He's changed my life in lots of ways: He's given me hope, purpose—eternity. He's forgiven me for all the stupid things I've ever done or thought. He's shown me what love—real love—is all about."

As I talk, and as this young waiter listens, I forget about the snow piling up outside—and tomorrow's big youth event. The only thing that seems to matter right now is this moment—and this person.

I talk, he listens—it's as simple as that. I don't use big words or debate lofty doctrines or worry about impressing this guy. I merely tell my story and give him a glimpse of my heart.

About thirty cups of coffee later, the waiter points to his watch. "It's getting late, and the weather looks pretty bad," he says. "I'll let you go so you can find a motel for the night. Thanks for talking with me. I've got a lot to think about."

I smile and shake his hand. "You asked some good questions. Don't stop doing that."

As I head out the door and trudge through the snow, hoping I said all the right things, I experience a kind of icy road awakening. *Lord, I get it. It's not just about "winning" someone's salvation. It's about genuinely "loving my neighbors." It's about keeping my heart on fire for you, so you can work through me. It's especially about living in a way that points others to eternity.*

I believe God put me on that highway and in that snow-storm—and eventually in that restaurant—just so I could share my faith with that young man. And I believe he orchestrated that whole scene so I could learn three essential keys to being his witness:

1. Have compassion on others—instead of treating nonbelievers as a project. "Jesus replied: 'Love the Lord your God with all your heart and with all your soul and with all your mind.' This is the first and greatest commandment. And the second is like it: 'Love your neighbor as yourself'" (Matt. 22:37–39).
2. Be prepared to speak up—instead of keeping quiet. "Always be prepared to give an answer to everyone who asks you to give the reason for the hope that you have" (1 Peter 3:15).
3. Allow the Holy Spirit to touch the world through you—instead of blending into the crowd. "Do your best to present yourself to God as one approved, a

workman who does not need to be ashamed and who correctly handles the word of truth" (2 Tim. 2:15).

And to be effective witnesses Christians need to . . .

KNOW what we believe and why by plugging into the Holy Bible daily. (We can't share with others what we don't know.)

BELIEVE what we know by trusting Jesus Christ daily. (We can't convince others of something we doubt.)

LIVE what we know and believe by consistently "practicing what we preach." (We can't tell people one thing, then live another way.)

Check Your Pulse

▸ What's your motive when you witness?
▸ Is your faith growing, or are you currently stagnate?
▸ Can others see Jesus in your lifestyle?

PART 3

KNOW HOW TO GROW

Reality Bytes

Faith on the Edge

I'm sick of being a wimpy Christian," fifteen-year-old Jason confesses to his buddies in discipleship group. "I act one way at church and around you guys, then another way with my friends at school. It's like . . . I don't even know who I am at times."

Jason's comments strike a nerve with the four other boys lounging on my living room floor. Chris and Andy, both sixteen, nod their heads in agreement, and fourteen-year-old Brian—who has been busy all evening stuffing his face with chips—perks up too.

"I know God doesn't like it when I act this way," Jason continues. "And I know I need to give up a few bad friendships so I can grow stronger as a Christian. But it's really hard."

Suddenly, a serious expression washes over Brian's face. "I'm with you, Jason," he says. "I've been a wimp about my faith. I've got some stuff to change in my life too."

Just as I'm about to jump in with a few words of encouragement, Chad—one of the older guys in the group—speaks up. "You're on the right track," the seventeen-year-old says. "Lose those friendships that are pulling you down. That's what I had to do.

"I used to care more about popularity than my faith," Chad continues. "Then one day I thought to myself, *It's stupid to follow the crowd at school. I'm a Christian. I'm different . . . and that's okay.*"

Jason sits up. "I've got it," he says with a grin. "Let's make a pact for purity. Let's help each other commit to a deeper faith in God."

I sit back and watch with amazement. *These guys are spurring each other on to a deeper walk with Christ,* I think to myself. *These boys are growing up!*

Let's Talk: Discussion Starter

It had taken three years for my discipleship group to reach a deep level of unity, openness, and trust. Three years of Bible studies, praying together, and crying with each other—not to mention all the pizza pig-outs, video marathons, and squirt gun wars we'd shared together.

In addition to being the editor of Focus on the Family's *Breakaway* magazine, I often lead teen discipleship groups at church. The guys from the group mentioned above are now in college, and I'm currently working with other teens. But I'll never forget watching those five awkward boys grow into solid men of God. We had taken seriously the challenge of growing deeper in our walk with Christ—and our effort paid off.

Together, we learned the importance of Bible reading, daily prayer, worship, tearing off our masks, and confessing our sins to Jesus—as well as to each other. We had discovered some keys to building a strong faith: choosing friends wisely, being the right kind of friend, handling hardships with a level head, and holding each other accountable to our commitments.

Now it's your turn. You're obviously hungry for the deeper stuff of God—that's why you're reading this book. As you plunge into the next section and learn some ways to grow in your faith and influence your peers, consider this Scripture passage:

> For God, who said, "Let light shine out of darkness," made his light shine in our hearts to give us the light of the knowledge of the glory of God in the face of Christ. But we have this treasure in jars of clay to show that this all-surpassing power is from God and not from us. . . . Therefore we do not lose heart. Though outwardly we are wasting away, yet inwardly we are being renewed day by day.
>
> 2 Corinthians 4:6–7, 16

▸ How can friends "make you" and "break you"?

▸ Read John 15:9–17. Name some qualities about Jesus that make him the ultimate best friend.

▸ Turn to Revelation and read these verses: 2:7, 11, 17, 26; 3:5, 12, 21. What does each tell you about the importance of finishing well?

▸ What is prayer and why is it important to pray? (For some clues, look up Rom. 8:26–27; Eph. 6:18; Phil. 4:4–7; Rev. 3:20.)

▸ What makes the Bible different from other collections of books?

▸ Those who followed Christ ended up being served by him. (Imagine that—the Creator *serving* his creation!) What's more, his disciples got a big dose of encouragement, mixed with some well-deserved correction from time to time. Jesus stretched his disciples as they struggled to receive the truth and obey the will of God. How do you think Jesus is going to stretch your life? What hope do you have of handling struggles that come your way?

▸ Name some ways you can reach out and serve the people in your group or church.

▸ How can your group or church serve your community?

Truth Encounters

Day 15: Bible Reading

How to Sword Fight

For the word of God is living and active. Sharper than any double-edged sword, it penetrates even to dividing soul and spirit, joints and marrow; it judges the thoughts and attitudes of the heart.

Hebrews 4:12

Get Real

Two glowing eyes are fixed on a girl reading her Bible.

A lanky demon blinks a couple of times, then rubs his scaly chin. He's unsure of what to do. The other hops wildly on two scrawny legs, unable to catch a glimpse into the girl's living room window. Both scramble for cover as their assigned target looks up and squints into the darkness.

"She's impossible," growls the puny one as he spits leaves from his mouth. "It's that weapon—she won't put it down."

"Silence!" his partner snaps. "Has someone stuck you with a pitchfork? Our master would eat us for a midnight snack if he heard you talk like that. We've got to find a way."

"She won't pay any attention to us," the little demon insists. "I bet she's studying her Bible right now." He sticks his head through the wall, confirming his suspicion. Then he jumps back, shivering. The enemy's book does that to him sometimes.

Suddenly, the tall demon slaps his forehead and begins to giggle like a jackal. "I've got it! Let's tempt her to live the Christian life by herself. We'll separate her from her pastor and church friends. Then we'll fill her mind with doubts about that wretched book she always reads."

"In three months, maybe six, our target will be so lonely and proud," the short fiend chuckles, "she'll fall flat on her face. Then she's all ours!"

The two demons huddle to plan their attack.

Question: What's living, active, and sharper than a two-edged sword? (If you read the Scripture passage at the beginning of today's lesson, you know what it is.)

Answer: That's right. It's the thick book you own with tons of words and not many pictures—the Holy Bible.

The Word of God is described as an offensive weapon (Eph. 6:17), which, if used properly, can help you win battles against the enemy, teach you about God's character, and equip you with the power you need to stand strong.

Question: If you don't care much about growing in your faith or winning battles against the enemy, what's the best strategy?

Answer: Let your sword gather dust on a shelf.

Flabby, shallow Christians simply hide their Bibles, are seen just enough at church and youth group to "keep others off their backs," and don't "waste energy" becoming the kind of holy people they really don't care to be.

Since you're reading this book, it's safe to say you're not satisfied with being a shallow Christian. You want to shape up. You want to learn to sword fight—and win!

It all begins with commitment: Starting right now, don't let a day pass without reading the Bible. (Agreed? Great!) Only the depth of God's Word can develop in you the depth of spirit you need to be a victorious Christian. So let's not waste any more time. Let the sword fighting lessons begin.

Get Ready

▸ **Isaiah 55** What does the Lord offer to those who seek him?

▸ **Ephesians 6:10–18** What is the armor of God?

▸ **2 Timothy 3:10–17** What is your greatest weapon in life?

Get Going

▸ **Use your sword daily.** Do you remember when you first became a Christian? I sure do. In fact, that unforgettable experience was a little like a roller-coaster ride.

First, I felt a rush of excitement and enthusiasm . . . and couldn't wait to tell the world about my new relationship with Jesus. Then, a few months down the road, I hit bottom and the zeal seemed to fade. When I was around my peers at school or work, I'd even catch myself feeling a bit embarrassed about what I believed.

I couldn't help scratching my head and wondering, *What happened?*

A warning from 1 Thessalonians 5:19 rang in my ears: "Do not put out the Spirit's fire." I soon learned that my "faith fire" was fizzling. Why? Because I wasn't fueling it. I wasn't spending time reading the Word . . . and acting upon it. And when my convictions were on the line and the pressure hit hard, I didn't have the strength to stand firm.

Make a commitment right now to set aside a portion of your day (at least five days a week) to study a few passages from the Bible—along with daily readings from a devotional guide like this one.

▸ **Learn the sword-fighting basics.** (1) Pray before you read Scripture. Ask the Holy Spirit to illuminate your mind and to help you understand the scriptural truths you'll encounter. (2) Don't attempt to read the Bible as you would a school textbook, racing through big blocks of type. The Holy Scriptures are unlike anything else you'll ever study. Every word is inspired by God. It's like a collection of personal letters written by our heavenly Father—just for us. Savor each word, rereading passages.

▸ **Carry your sword into battle.** God's holy words can empower your life if you do two things: memorize and apply. As you read through the Bible each day, highlight a passage or two and begin committing them to memory.

Day 16: Prayer

Invited by the King

The eyes of the LORD are on the righteous
and his ears are attentive to their cry.

Psalm 34:15

Get Real

The king sits alone in his royal chamber, waiting—even though there is an endless line of ambassadors to greet, laws to enact, an evil sorcerer to banish.

Glancing up from a list of names and focusing on a large cedar door, he smiles. Yes, there is a lot to do. But first some subjects are stopping by for a private visit—some very important subjects he has invited. At least *he* thinks they are important.

The door opens and in comes a beautiful young woman dressed in the finest quality gown money can buy. Without acknowledging the king's smile or outstretched hand, the girl falls to her knees, then focuses her eyes on the ceiling.

"O thou great and merciful king who art in the grandest of all castles . . . in the grandest of all lands," the lady babbles without taking a breath. "O thou in whom so much doth dwell, upon whose crown hath been placed much authority, incline thine ear toward thy most humble subject. Keep thine subject eternally safe in thy splendid kingdom."

"Get up at once," encourages the king. "I want to gaze upon your face and hear what's really on your heart, not empty words—"

"Thanks and good-bye," the girl interrupts, seeming not to hear. Then she spins around and trots out of the chamber.

The king sighs. Why did it always seem to go like this?

"Next, please," he says, motioning to his attendant.

A tall knight-in-training struts in—completely decked out in a shiny suit of armor. The boy also ignores the king's greeting.

"Your royal highness," he declares as he slides off his helmet, "there's this amazingly gorgeous maiden I met while riding through Sherwood Forest the other day . . . and I want to ask her to the annual ball this weekend. But I think she needs a little 'royal' persuasion. Know what I mean? You can see to it that she doesn't say no. Now this is important!"

The king clears his throat politely. "Speaking of important," he ventures, "how do you feel about my efforts to help the poor? Would you like to have a part in—"

"And another thing!" the young man continues. "I misplaced my sword. I can't be a real knight without a sword. Now, you find it for me, okay? Well, later."

With that the knight-in-training slides on his helmet and marches out the door. The king slumps on his throne. "Next," he says.

This time when the door opens there seems to be no one there. Then the king looks down and sees a quivering child peeking into the massive chamber. The boy enters shyly, his eyes wide.

"Are . . . are you *really* the king?" the child asks.

The king smiles warmly. "I really am," he answers, offering his hand.

The little boy reaches up and shakes it. Then he climbs into a plump, over-stuffed chair, folds his arms, and waits.

The king watches, amazed, as the boy sits politely for nearly a minute. "Isn't there something you wanted to tell me?" the king asks finally. "Something you have to recite—some kind of demand, perhaps?"

The little boy looks down for a moment, thinking, then looks up. "Yes," he says, "I guess there is."

"Go ahead—speak your mind."

"Thank you for inviting me. That's all."

When the king hears this, he can't seem to say anything for a while. All he can do is smile.

But then the two talk and talk and talk for the longest, most wonderful time.

Do you talk regularly to the eternal King—God? Hold on . . . I mean really talk *to* him, not *at* him. Are your talks more than a feeble attempt to "do your duty" with canned, programmed expressions that sound nice?

In Joshua 1:5 the Lord says, "I will never leave you nor forsake you." God is the King who listens. He has extended his hand to you and invites you to share whatever is on your mind—anytime, anywhere.

Get Ready

> ▸ **Proverbs 15:29** Based on this verse, what could end up hindering your prayers?
> ▸ **Matthew 6:5–13** What must you do when you pray?
> ▸ **James 5:13–18** What is the prayer of a righteous person?

Get Going

▸ **Know what prayer is.** Prayer is not just going through the motions, saying a bunch of thoughtless, mechanical words—as some people do when they give thanks for a meal. It is actually communicating with the one and only eternal God. "He is the incredible God who created everything there is, and who is in control of the universe, which is expanding at the rate of 186,000 miles a second in all directions every hour," writes Kenneth N. Taylor in his book *How to Grow*. (Kenneth is a popular scholar who is famous for translating *The Living Bible*.) "You, as God's child, can come right into His presence where He joyfully welcomes you because you have become His."

▸ **Stop making excuses—just do it!** It amazes me when I hear Christian teens (or adults) make lame excuses such as, "I don't know what to say," or "I don't know how to pray!" If you've figured out how to talk to a friend on the phone or how to send e-mail on the Internet, then you know how to pray. Jesus is your best friend, and he wants you to tell him about everything that's going on in your life. He wants to know the desires of your heart, how badly you feel when you fail, how happy you are when good things happen—*everything!* And while the Bible tells us to pray always and for any reason (see Eph. 6:18), Jesus has also demonstrated the importance of getting alone to pray (see Matt. 26:36–39.)

▸ **Get alone with God.** Find a private place *anywhere*—your bedroom, the kitchen table while everyone else is asleep, an undisturbed corner of your school's library—and carve out a block of "quiet time" every day for prayer. Exactly what time you do this and for how long is up to you. I prefer early mornings (for usually about twenty to thirty minutes) in my home office. The key is to spend some time alone with God so that you can give him your undivided attention. A committed, unhurried quiet time is actually the most important part of a Christian's day.

It's your time to . . .

> let go of your fears and worries.
> listen to God's instruction.
> praise your awesome Creator.
> pray for friends and family.
> power up with the Holy Spirit.

Day 17: Confession

God Sees All

If we confess our sins, he is faithful and just and will forgive us our sins and purify us from all unrighteousness.

1 John 1:9

Get Real

Laurissa smiles at the Wal-Mart greeter then heads straight to the jewelry section. She circles the watch counter but isn't really interested in buying a new Timex. She's here for a different reason.

Her eyes cautiously survey the cashier's station as she pretends to be interested in a silver chain. As usual, the store is buzzing with activity. *Not yet,* Laurissa tells herself. *Too risky.*

She patiently sorts through a rack full of gaudy, seventies-style beads, occasionally stopping and holding up a strand—just to maintain her act, of course. After what feels like an eternity, Laurissa sees her chance. A short distance away, a man is pointing at a diamond engagement ring, and the cashier is jamming key after key into a lock, trying to figure out which one will open the case.

Now!

Like a wolf attacking its next meal, Laurissa swiftly pounces on a pair of crystal earrings—the ones her mom insists aren't worth $18.95. *No security tags—good! That means no annoying alarms!*

Without a second thought, Laurissa quickly slides the earrings into her purse—undetected. And to ensure her cover, Laurissa pays for a $2.99 strand of lime-green beads. *Perfect for Seventies Day at school.*

"Thanks, miss," the cashier says as she hands Laurissa her receipt.

"No, thank *you*," Laurissa says with a grin.

Before long, she's out the door and is standing by her parents' minivan—completely relieved. Just as Laurissa digs into her purse and begins poking around for her keys, a sharp voice startles her from behind. "Excuse me, young lady!"

Laurissa spins around and locks eyes with a middle-aged housewife. Only, this housewife is flashing a badge. "I'm with store security," the lady says bluntly, "and I'll have to ask you to step back inside."

A few minutes later, Laurissa's stomach begins to churn as she sits in front of a TV monitor, saying everything was a big mistake. Yet right there, before a store clerk, a manager, and the undercover security woman, Laurissa can see her criminal act in living color. It was all so vivid. A hidden video camera had caught every one of her clever moves.

"Okay," Laurissa says as she plucks the earrings from her purse and hands them to the store manager. "I did it—you got your woman. I'm totally guilty."

A tear rolls down her cheek. *Stealing, lying—how could I be so stupid? And what's gonna happen now? Is my life ruined?*

I doubt there's a person alive who hasn't thought he could get away with something because no one would see him. Guess what? God sees every action and hears every word. Though he's quick to offer forgiveness when we ask for it, one thing is sure: We can't hide from God—not now, not ever.

Is integrity important to you? Deep down inside, do you want to do what's right and pleases God? If you just nodded yes—great! But keep in mind that nearly every day you're faced with choices that show the world, and God, your honest answer. The temptation to steal, to stretch the truth (or tell only half of it), and to cheat, is always staring you in the face. Unless you consciously decide to make integrity a priority, sin will push you over the line, as it did with Laurissa.

It's like a tug-of-war is going on inside you. Your old nature is still there, and if you give it a chance by encouraging it, it sort of takes control. The result: a strained relationship with God.

So how do you make things right again? Answer: It all starts with confession.

Get Ready

▸ **Psalm 51** If we sin, what must we do?
▸ **Psalm 103** How can we know for sure that Jesus forgives our sin?
▸ **1 John 2:1–14** How is God's Word made complete in us?

Get Going

▸ **Restore your relationship by admitting the mistake.** Take a long, honest look at sin in your life, then tell Jesus Christ that you're sorry (make sure you mean it). Once you've confessed the sin and asked him to help you change (called repentance), you can stop flogging yourself. You're totally forgiven. Now with your relationship fully restored with God, you can take steps toward growth and change. (The Holy Spirit will help you.)

▸ **Know the truth.** A pure mind is not a mind free of temptation. A pure mind chooses to act in the right way when temptation strikes. Or, put another way, temptation is inevitable; what counts is how you meet it. Keep in mind that a person can be good without being faithful, and faithful without being good. What will it take for you to combine both?

a. A stronger desire to be good.

b. A greater sense that faithfulness will be rewarded.

c. Friends who have the same goal.

d. A swift kick in the pants.

e. Confessing past wrongs to God, so you can start over.

f. Another person or two to help you stay on track on a weekly basis.

Answer: While each is important, *e* is the first and most important step.

▸ **Examine Matthew 25:14–30.** Try to imagine one day seeing Jesus Christ face-to-face. Do you want to hear him say to you, "Well done, good and faithful servant"?

Day 18: Hardships

Screamin' Down a Wacky Track

We are hard pressed on every side, but not crushed; perplexed, but not in despair; persecuted, but not abandoned; struck down, but not destroyed.

2 Corinthians 4:8–9

Get Real

I squeeze my eyes shut and grip the safety bar. "EEEEEYYOOOWEEEE!!!"

Seconds after takeoff, the Zambezi Zinger launches into "whiplash mode," blasting around treacherous twists and turns and stretching my face into a dozen different contortions. A ton of catastrophic possibilities race through my mind: *We're goin' too fast. We're not gonna make the next curve. We're history!*

Suddenly, the roller coaster slows, then begins a steep, spiral ascent. I take a deep breath and glance at my friend Marty.

"Awesome coaster, isn't it?" he says, giving me a quick high five.

I flash a forced grin. "Sorry, but my stomach doesn't agree."

"Hey, we're just gettin' started," Marty says. "There's lots more ahead. This is sort of the calm before the storm—so hold on."

Calm before the storm?! More ahead?!

Once at the top, the roller coaster comes to a jerking stop. I glance over the edge. For half a millisecond the park looks kinda peaceful, but then it happens. The mean machine begins its bone-jarring plunge . . . and the world becomes distorted.

"Uh-oh," I mumble. "This time, there's no way we're gonna make it. This time, we're . . . EEEEEYY-OOOWEEEE!!!"

Loop, lunge, plunge, zip, flip, whirl—if your stomach can hold up, it's an awesome feeling having your mind rattled and your body flung in a zillion directions. But when your life starts to feel like a roller coaster, that's a different matter!

Just when we feel as if we're on top of the world, just when everything seems to be cruising along perfectly . . . our lives plunge into trouble—usually when we least expect it. But as Christians, we know who's in control of this big roller coaster ride of life: Jesus Christ.

Our Lord doesn't stay back at the station. He goes with us on the ride—always taking care of us no matter what's around the next turn. And after every low point in life, Jesus gives us another high. "He has delivered us from such a deadly peril, and he will deliver us. On him we have set our hope that he will continue to deliver us" (2 Cor. 1:10).

Here's something else I've discovered about life: Most of our greatest triumphs come out of a very difficult, wilderness-type experience. Even as Christians, our lives will be full of valleys *and* mountaintops. We are not promised a way around them—but a way *through* them. And once we go through, we always come out stronger than before.

So hold tight to your faith when times get tough. Life is tough, but Jesus is tougher.

Get Ready

- ▸ **John 14:15–27** How will Christ comfort us in times of trouble?
- ▸ **2 Corinthians 4:1–18** What gives us hope during hard times?
- ▸ **Philippians 3:1–11** What must we focus on during good times and bad?

Get Going

▸ **Sometimes the only way God can bless you is by breaking you.** Hardships are not easy, and they're not fun. You feel alone, unaware that you might, in fact, be very close to an encounter with God. This may be how he's getting your attention. A friend once told me, "God whispers in our pleasure, but he shouts in our pain."

▸ **Struggling is not a sign of weakness.** Dead things don't struggle! Struggle is a sign of life!

▸ **Jesus shares your pain.** He puts himself in your shoes and feels everything that you feel. He is the Father of "suffering with" and the God of all comfort! And when he comes beside you and offers you the strength to take the next step, you learn to walk with fellow sufferers—to let their pain become your pain.

▸ **Feelings do not equal faith.** Your faith is based on the unchangeable truth that God came to earth in the person of Jesus, died for your sins, rose again from the dead, and even today reigns as Lord over all. Nothing can change this truth—not feelings, not indigestion, not bad hair days, not lousy school days.

Day 19: Friendships

Power of the Pack

As iron sharpens iron,
  so one man sharpens another.

Proverbs 27:17

Get Real

Snapshot 1

Brian jogs along the shore with his buddies. The day is absolutely awesome. The sun beats down on his shoulders, the surf laps at his feet, and . . . WHOA! . . . the beach is filled with miles of gorgeous sun goddesses.

The sixteen-year-old has trouble keeping his eyes on the surf. And his pals don't make it any easier. They whistle, pop off with endless catcalls, and crack one crude joke after another. Brian even joins in a few times.

Then his stomach knots up and a chilling thought shoots through his mind: *Wait a minute . . . I'm a Christian! I'm not supposed to act this way. What's happening to me? I think I'm goin' crazy!*

Snapshot 2

Fourteen-year-old Rebecca has a tough choice to make.

It's Friday night, and she's lounging on her bedroom floor, listening to music with her two best friends, Shelly and Meg. Shelly wants to smoke some marijuana she got from her older sister. Meg suggests they wash it down with a bottle of red wine she has hidden in her backpack.

Rebecca's parents are gone for the evening. No one will find out.

"Don't wimp out," Shelly says as she lights a joint. "It's not like you're gonna turn into a druggie."

Rebecca punches up the volume on her stereo and fiddles with the equalizer—anything to avoid eye contact. Deep in her gut, she's scared. She has never considered using drugs, especially since she asked Christ into her life. And she never imagined that friends from *church* would be the ones tempting her.

Lord, what should I do? she prays. *These are my friends.*

Friends. The right ones will get in your face when you're blowing it, pull you up when you're down, and even put your best interests first. And the wrong ones? Let's just say I've seen too many lives destroyed because of stupid decisions—and the power of the pack.

It's hard to make it on your own as a Christian. That's why fostering the right friendships is an essential key to growing in your faith. Check out these verses:

> Two are better than one,
> because they have a good return for their work:
> If one falls down,
> his friend can help him up.

Ecclesiastes 4:9–10

A friend loves at all times.

Proverbs 17:17

Wounds from a friend can be trusted.

Proverbs 27:6

Friends who pull you down, stab you in the back, leech onto you during the good times then split the scene when you need help aren't friends at all. It's time to lose these kinds of leeching losers.

A good friend . . .

accepts you despite all your miserable blunders.
allows you to take off your mask and feel safe.
makes you feel special, valuable, gifted, loved.
moves you toward greatness.

Get Ready

▸ **Psalm 133** How should friends live?
▸ **Proverbs 27:1–10** What's the mark of a true friend?
▸ **John 15:9–17** What sets apart Christ's friends from his enemies?

Get Going

▸ **Take inventory of your friendships.** Do you find yourself following the crowd—just to stay with the in crowd? Is popularity more important than genuine friendship?

If your friends are leading you in the wrong direction, and you continue to follow, beware: You're not living your life anymore—the crowd is. (And when it comes time to pay the price for your actions, you end up doing it all by yourself.)

▸ **Sever bad ties—before you get tied up.** When God says one thing in the Bible and your friends say another, then you must follow God and let your friends leave you if they wish. It's a hard choice, but one Christians sometimes have to make.

▸ **Unplug peer pressure.** Build a set of values right now and think about your actions *before* you get in a tight spot. Weigh the consequences of your decisions before you act, and find the hidden dangers before they sneak up on you. This is one of the best defenses you can develop. By preplanning your response and having your values set beforehand, you are more prepared to act as you want to act—not as the group wants you to act.

▸ **Seek Christian friends who share your values.** And spend less time with friends who aren't interested in pursuing a godly walk. Like it or not, the people you spend time with have a big influence on your life. If your pals are doing things you know are wrong, don't let them drag you down too. You might even consider not hanging out with them.

Day 20: Trust

Caught in a Crosscurrent

Fear not, for I have redeemed you;
  I have summoned you by name; you are mine.
When you pass through the waters,
  I will be with you.

Isaiah 43:1–2

Get Real

I grip my bodyboard and bob patiently in the churning surf off Southern California's Huntington Beach. I gaze over my shoulder and squint—scanning the horizon for the right wave.

Suddenly, I shoot into action, beating the water with my arms and kicking to propel myself.

"I got it, I got it!" I scream. "WHAAAAAAHOOO!!"

My timing is perfect—finally! The last few waves have left me tumbling helplessly in the ocean's depths. (Okay, I admit it . . . I'm not a skilled bodyboarder, but I love the sport anyway.)

I catch the lip of a respectable wave rising beneath me and soon experience the "slide ride" I've been seeking. I rocket atop the curl like a missile homing in on a target and ride it toward shore.

Several waves later, as the surf begins to mellow, a friend and I decide to kick back on our bodyboards and soak up the summer sun. Big mistake. We dangle our legs and arms in the warm Pacific water, not even considering the riptides and crosscurrents around us.

Soon, my buddy and I are floating a billion light years from reality—lost in crazy conversation and lots of laughs. Next stop: Hawaii!

"Uh—hey, man," I say, looking toward shore, "I think we're drifting."

"It's your imagination," my friend laughs. "The water is really calm right now. Besides, we can still see our section of the beach."

"No," I insist, "I think we've strayed too far. Look at the people. They're getting smaller. And look at the lifeguards—I think they're motioning at us!"

We both begin to paddle with all our strength but seem to be on a watery treadmill. We don't move an inch.

"It's like we're trapped in a current," my friend gasps.

"That's exactly right," I shout. "We're caught in a crosscurrent. Paddle harder!"

I look up again and spot the lifeguards swimming toward us.

How humiliating! I tell myself. *I practically grew up in the ocean. I just can't be rescued! I'll never live it down.*

Before I have time to think about the consequences, I hop off my board and dig my arms into the water—determined to make it out of this jam on my own. But the harder I swim, the more exhausted I become.

"Come on, man," my friend says, as he hops off his board and begins to swim like crazy. "Don't give up. We can make it to shore."

Every muscle begins to cramp. I choke on a mouthful of seawater, go under, then surface again. Suddenly, raw fear surges through my body. "I can't do it," I yell. "I need help—"

I go under once more, kick my legs harder, and manage to stick my head above water. I open my eyes to a now welcomed sight: the lifeguard's hand reaching out to me.

With every ounce of strength within me, I fling my arm up and grasp it. "Praise, God—I'm saved!"

My friend and I will never forget that day at the beach—especially how two quick-thinking lifeguards turned near-disaster into victory.

As I stood on the shore watching other bodyboarders shred the surf, the scene replayed in my mind. *The ocean is deceptive,* I thought. *Even when it looks safe, dangerous currents lurk below the surface. And no matter how hard we fight with the water, we just can't make it on our own. We need a lifeguard.*

Our faith is like that too. One minute we're rocketing through life on a smooth course. The next minute we're caught in a crosscurrent—and pounded by pressure: friends who pull us down, parents and teachers who heap on high expectations . . . doubts, fears, stubbornness.

The good news is, we have a Lifeguard.

Christ will pull us out of any trouble we face. He's extending his hand. We need to grasp it and trust him.

Get Ready

> ▸ **Psalm 20** Where must we put our trust?
> ▸ **Isaiah 25:1–26:4** Why must we trust the Lord?
> ▸ **Mark 10:13–16** How must we trust Jesus?

Get Going

> ▸ **Understand three truths.** (1) You can't swim against the tide of God and survive. But you can come to

the surface and cry out, "Abba, Father," and he'll set you on the right course. (2) Not one person on this planet is outside the reach of God's love. (3) Even if you can't begin to fathom the depth of your sin—Jesus understands. And he forgives you.

▸ **Know whom to trust.** One of my favorite authors, Max Lucado, has a simple strategy for trusting God. In his book *He Still Moves Stones,* Max writes: "Take Jesus at His word. Learn that when He says something, it happens. When He says we're forgiven, let's unload the guilt. When He says we're valuable, let's believe Him. When He says we're provided for, let's stop worrying."

▸ **Ask God for help.** Pray something like this: "Lord, teach me how to trust with the quiet, unquestioning trust of a little child. And give me an extra measure of peace that you're protecting me—and that you'll do the right thing in every situation. I'm taking your hand right now, and I'm trusting you. Amen."

Day 21: Worship

Are You a High-Voltage Christian?

Yet a time is coming and has now come when the true worshipers will worship the Father in spirit and truth, for they are the kind of worshipers the Father seeks.

John 4:23

Get Real

"What do you mean you don't want to come to youth group tonight?!" Kathy asks. "You promised you would this time."

Jeff takes a sip of Coke, fidgets with his French fries, then looks across the table at Kathy. "I just don't get into all that singing and clapping and 'lifting up your hands' . . . and all that other stuff your youth pastor tells everybody to do."

"It's called worship," Kathy says.

"Yeah, well, it's not my style," Jeff insists. "Why can't you accept me the way I am? I'll follow God my way—you do it your way."

Kathy's face suddenly turns red. Her plan is backfiring—again.

Going out for a burger always seems to get Jeff's attention. But the minute she brings up church or youth group and the possibility of their attending together, her boyfriend comes up with a million excuses.

Jeff leans forward and locks eyes with Kathy. "Look, I attended winter retreat 'cause you asked me to," he says. "You prayed with me and I even accepted Jesus in my life! And that was great. Then you and I started dating—and that was even better. I just don't need church, okay? But I do need you."

"Don't you see how twisted that is, Jeff?" Kathy asks. "You don't just say a few 'magic words' to God, then go off and do what you want. Your commitment to Jesus has to be real. You have to mean it—then live it. And you have to live it his way—not yours."

"Oh, wonderful," Jeff says, flopping back in his chair. "Here comes your youth pastor's favorite guilt-filled sermon. I've heard it before, you know. Read my lips: I just don't fit your neat, little mold of how a Christian is supposed to act."

Jeff pauses, takes another sip of his Coke, and looks up again. "I'm not a phony. My faith *is* real."

"If that's true, then grow it," Kathy says. "I'm not forcing you to fit a mold. It's just that you oughta take a lesson from the soccer games you watch."

"Soccer! What?"

"Soccer, basketball, hockey . . . whatever. You never miss a game on TV. And when you watch them, you raise your arms and scream for your favorite team, right?"

"Yeah," Jeff says with a blank stare.

"You also get excited when you go to concerts—and yell and sing and dance around a lot, right?"

"Sure."

"You even flatter me with kind words—and tell me how much you love me."

"And I mean it," Jeff says. "But how does this have anything to do with faith?"

"My point is, I don't see you doing any of these things for God," Kathy says, taking Jeff's hand. "If you love Jesus as much as you love sports or music or me, then show it. You don't have to scream and jump around at church. Just be there. And make sure your heart is there too. That's what worship is all about."

A grin stretches across Jeff's face. "Good sermon. No guilt," he says. "I'll come to youth group tonight. Not for you. I'll do it for him."

Worshiping God is an interactive experience. "Come near to God and he will come near to you" (James 4:8).

It's both private and public. It involves your heart and your head. And as you linger in God's presence, praising him, it's like you get a high-voltage spiritual zap. Worship builds you into a stronger Christian.

As you worship God, you should . . .

> give him your praise and glory.
> give him your thanks.
> give him your whole heart.

As you worship God, you shouldn't . . .

> go through the motions of an empty ritual.
> approach him with wrong motives, using your
>   praise as a means of getting something.
> treat this special time as an option in your life.

You're God's awesome creation, and he wants your worship. It pleases him and plugs your life into the ultimate power source. And if you stay plugged in, those high-voltage spiritual zaps will gradually transform you into a high-voltage Christian!

But be warned: If you don't make worship a priority, your Christian walk will be shallow and ineffective.

The choice is yours.

Get Ready

> ▶ **Psalm 63** Based on this passage, how would you define *worship*?
>
> ▶ **John 4:1–26** How do true worshipers worship God?
>
> ▶ **2 Corinthians 3:17–18** What transforms our lives?

Get Going

> ▶ **Rate your worship.** Answer the following questions:
>
> True/False. My interest in faith is equal to other interests in my life: relationships with the opposite sex, sports, music.
>
> True/False. My church's services bore me to death.
>
> True/False. Sometimes I go weeks without praying.
>
> True/False. God often seems distant to me.

If you answered true to even one of the above questions, you need to ask yourself a few questions: Is God the most important person in my life . . . or am I allowing other pursuits to push him out of my life? Is church really boring . . . or am I just too tired to participate? Do

I truly expect God to speak to me during a worship service . . . or am I just going through the motions?

▸ **Quench your thirst.** Go back and reread John 4:1–26. Remember the kind of worshiper God seeks? (Hint: The kind who worships him in spirit and truth.) Remember what Jesus offers. (Here's another hint: living water.) Like most Christians, your faith can get pretty dry at times. But the living water Jesus gives can transform the most desolate, desertlike soul into an abundant life spring!

▸ **Get wired for worship.** True, not every church service will be filled with fireworks, but you can make worship more meaningful by doing two things: (1) Ask God to prepare your heart *before* you step through the church doors. Tell him that you really want to focus on him and deepen your faith. (2) Ask God to help you make knowing him the priority in your life. This means spending time daily reading the Bible, praying, and worshiping him.

Salt and Light

Christ in the Classroom

"Hey, Bible boy. Where's your Word?" shouts a voice from across the crowded hall.

Fifteen-year-old Eric Stueberg grins and holds up a tattered black leather book with fluorescent white words—HOLY BIBLE—handwritten across the cover.

"Right here," he says. "Wouldn't leave home without it!"

It's Monday morning at Florida's Fort Walton Beach High School, and Eric loves his new reputation. While other teens return from the weekend bragging about how far they went sexually or how much they had to drink, Eric can't stop boasting about his radical God . . . and how far Christ can take a life that's fired up for him.

It all started when Eric and some of his church friends realized they had work to do for God—starting with their own lives.

"During one of our revival services at Brownsville Assembly of God, the Lord came and poured his Spirit out on our church. It was amazing," Eric says. "And when the pastor invited people to the altar, my friends and I knew we needed to go forward."

The message from Revelation 3:15–16—about being lukewarm—had touched a nerve. Eric realized that he wasn't on track with Jesus and that attending church on Sundays and Wednesdays wasn't enough.

"You have to *know* Jesus," Eric says. "He has to be your best friend—your Lord.

"I thought about how half my school wasn't saved," Eric continues. "I knew I needed to make a change in my life, then reach out to other teens. I finally stood up and went down to the altar. Everything just broke. It was a real turnaround."

One of the first things Eric and his friend Julie Bronson did was start a Bible study at school. The second—and most important, he says—was to step out as a "walking billboard."

"Some teens wear Christian T-shirts and go to church, but they also spend their weekends partying," Eric says. "I used to be that way too. But I've seen how it can completely ruin a Christian's witness."

Today, he's convinced that if you're gonna claim to be Christian, you'd better live like one. After all, being a walking billboard means having your life read by others. "I want people to read 'Jesus' when they see me," he says. "That's why I love being called Bible boy. It's cool."

But being radical for God comes at a cost. Eric lost a few friends who thought he'd become too religious, and he occasionally gets picked on. "Let's not kid ourselves; taking a stand for God is far from easy," Eric says. "But who says following Jesus should be easy?"

The first few weeks were the hardest. But, gradually, casual friends began calling him Bible boy—with a positive tone—and some even visited his campus Bible study. The handful of teens who would spend their lunch hour praying was soon replaced by a roomful of teens.

"This world needs bold Christians," Eric says, "especially teenagers who are willing to stand in the face of what's popular and say, 'Jesus is the *only* truth, the *only* life, and the *only* way.'

"As far as being rejected, I don't want to stand before God on judgment day and hear the words, 'I counted on you to tell your friends about me, but you didn't.' I don't want my friends to spend eternity in hell. I can't be selfish. I've got to speak up . . . and do my part to rock my school for Christ."

Now that you've learned some ways to grow in your faith and stand strong, are you ready to reach out and turn your school "right side up" for God? Here are some ideas that Eric and his friends recommend.

▸ Start a campus Bible study. Meet with other Christians each morning before classes begin. Once your group gets off the ground, extend regular invitations to a kid who is on the fringes.

▸ Build up others. Don't give in to putting others down, even if you're just trying to have fun. The fact is, cuts, slams, and jabs hurt—deeply. Put-downs weaken a person's self-confidence and often don't heal for many years—if ever. Be the kind of Christian who builds up the body of Christ.

▸ Watch your witness. Living a double life is a surefire way to destroy trust and blow your witness. The fact is, Satan would love to convince nonbelievers that acting on God's standards is too tough, too demanding, and too stupid if they care to have a social life. And he'd love to trip you up just to prove his point. Don't let the enemy have a foothold.

But on the flip side of the coin, never be afraid to admit your weaknesses. It's okay to admit that your actions don't always match your convictions. Too often we think that by saying the words "I blew it" we somehow become weaker. Actually, just the opposite is true. Most people admire someone who has the courage to admit his or her mistakes.

▸ Have a servant's heart. I like what author F. B. Meyer explains in his book *Devotional Commentary:* "Serve others with a brave heart, looking up to Jesus—who for many years toiled at the carpenter's bench. Amid the many scenes and actions of life, set the Lord always before your face. Do all as in His presence, and to win His smile; and be sure to cultivate a spirit of love to God and man. Look out for opportunities of cheering your fellow-workers . . . so the lowliest service will glisten."

Check Your Pulse

▸ Name some well-intentioned witnessing methods that can end up backfiring—even making Christians look bad.

▸ Why is building a friendship with someone often the best first step toward telling him or her about God?

▸ If you had a chance to share your faith in the classroom—either through a term paper or a speech—what would be your primary motive: to impress the teacher, win a debate . . . or uncover the truth?

PART 4

KNOW WHERE YOU'RE GOING

Reality Bytes

Faith for the Future

Brett Newton thrashes about in the darkness, tugging at a seat belt twisted around his chest. But he can't get free. He gasps for air—he can't breathe.

The fifteen-year-old is trapped underwater—in the back of an overturned car.

I can't hold out. I'm gonna die!

He gasps for another breath—and chokes. He pounds on a window, then yanks harder at the seat belt.

Somebody, anybody . . . I'm trapped. Help! Please, please . . . H-E-L-P!

Brett throws off the covers and bolts up, his heart racing. He rubs his eyes, then focuses on a Chicago Bulls poster above his bed. Sweat rolls down his neck.

I'm in bed, Brett consoles himself. *I'm at home . . . in my own room. It was just a—*

The blond, curly haired teen shudders. If only it were a dream.

Why'd it have to happen? Why were my friends taken? And why was I spared?

Nine months earlier (December 1993), Brett was in a freak accident near his home in Redding, California.

While he walked away without a scratch, that wasn't the case for his two best friends—Scott and Daron Grubbs.

Their car rolled off a narrow bridge and overturned into the chilly water below. Scott, sixteen, drowned shortly after impact. Fourteen-year-old Daron, Scott's brother, died two days later at a local hospital.

"Daron and I were especially close," Brett says. "I stayed with him to the end. I miss him a lot."

Since the accident, the details have played out again and again in Brett's mind. Sometimes, the frightening scenes invade his sleep. "In my dreams, I'm usually the one struggling to live," he says. "That's not exactly how it happened."

Rendezvous with Disaster

It was New Year's Eve, and Scott, Daron, and Brett had just left a party for their youth group at Valley Christian Fellowship.

Brett climbed into the back of the "Mello Yellow Monster"—Scott's ever popular '78 Ford Maverick. Daron slid into the front. The guys decided to head off to a friend's house and continue their marathon of videos, munchies, and laughs. The fun was just beginning—or so they thought.

Since none of the guys had a clue how to find their next stop—and the wooded roads were dark and twisty—they followed close behind another carload of teens.

"Come on, Scott," Daron said. "Let's get moving—we're gonna lose 'em."

Scott accelerated, but the car ahead disappeared around a bend. Suddenly, as the guys neared the bridge that crosses Oak Run Creek, the car skidded out of control. Scott cranked the wheel—HARD—but it was too late.

CRU-U-UNCH . . . SPLASH!

"The next thing I knew, we flipped right over the edge and landed upside down," Brett says.

While the creek was calm and somewhat shallow (less than four feet deep), within seconds the front end of the "Monster" was completely submerged. Scott and Daron were both underwater and unconscious.

As for Brett, "It's a miracle I'm alive today," he says. "My seat belt was wrapped around my body and I was trapped, but I could still breathe. The back end of the car was above water."

The guys were trapped for less than thirty minutes. To Brett, it felt like an eternity.

"Scott and Daron were quiet the whole time," Brett says. "When help arrived and someone flashed a light inside, I could see an outline of the guys' limp bodies— and their hair floating in the water.

"At that moment, I was sure my friends had died . . . and that really freaked me out."

Brothers on Both Sides of Life

More than 130 teens and adults gathered at Mercy Hospital, where the guys were taken. Scott's friend Trisha Wheeler, sixteen, was one of them.

"It was the toughest thing I'd ever had to deal with," Trisha says. "I stayed at the hospital until Daron died. In the days that followed, I constantly asked, 'Why, God? Why did my friends have to die?'"

Brett was uninjured but in major shock. "It was difficult to understand," he says. "One minute we were laughing and having fun. Then the next, we were being rushed to a hospital. It makes you realize that our lives can come to an end at any time."

Hardest hit were Scott and Daron's parents, Bill and Krys. "Suddenly, you question everything you believe, and your faith is on the line," Krys says. "But Jesus is getting us through. And as Christians, we know our sons are home with the Lord."

Bill adds, "A few months before he died, Scott said he was going to be part of a revival in the youth."

"It has already started," Krys says. "Their friends are turning to the Lord. I believe that's a purpose in their deaths."

Gettin' Radical

A few months before the accident, Scott had made a decision about his life as a Christian: *It's all or nothing. No more goin' through the motions.*

His pastor had been talking about revival, and a few of his wise Sunday morning words stuck deep inside: "Christians who stay in their comfortable little religious boxes will never see revival. . . . But you can make a difference in the lives of others. God has work for you; now get going!"

Scott knew he had to fix his own walk—which he sometimes thought of as a limp crawl. But once he got on the right track, he began to reach out. Scott started with two of his closest friends and football buddies—Richard Dennis and Chad Franklin.

"He told us that football, parties, and popularity didn't matter to him anymore," Richard says. "He explained that only one thing counted in life: committing your heart to Jesus and living for him."

Chad adds, "Then he did something I'll never forget: He hugged us and said, 'I love you.' In the weeks ahead, I began to see a cool change in him, and I never respected anyone more than I respected him."

Next, Scott quit the football team at Foothill High School, where he attended.

"I was shocked when he came to me with his decision," says his coach, Mark Pettengill. "I looked him in the eyes and said, 'Scott, you're very talented—Why?' His answer shocked me even more: 'Because I need to spend the time getting closer to God.'"

Sparking a Campfire

In the days ahead, Scott was never seen at school without his Bible. And he was always decked out in blue jeans and a white T-shirt. He'd tell everyone he met, "White stands for purity."

"He really desired to be a godly guy and a solid example to others," says Mike Cleary, youth pastor at Valley Christian Fellowship. "Daron began to follow in his brother's footsteps.

"But trust me, they never stopped being a couple of zany guys. Whenever you saw the two, they'd have giant smiles stretched across their faces, or they'd pop off with jokes."

In school, many students and faculty began to take notice of Scott's radical new walk. According to Lisa Fredrick, an English teacher at Foothill High (and a Christian who helped Scott start a lunch-hour Bible study), Scott was a committed clique buster.

"He didn't hang out with just the popular people," she says. "He befriended everybody—especially the underdogs. People really respected him for that."

Trisha says Scott and his brother would even spend time at a local soup kitchen, witnessing to the homeless. "God put a flame in Scott," Trisha explains. "And Scott shared it with his brother, Daron. Through the two of them, it grew. And as they shared with others, it turned into a campfire . . . and just kept right on growing. Today, Scott's flame is a bonfire."

Let's Talk: Discussion Starter

While a town mourned the loss of two solid young men, it also celebrated the legacy of faith that was left behind.

God put a flame in Scott and Daron, and that flame touched hundreds of other teens. Both boys discovered something that takes many people a lifetime to learn: A Christian's most important pursuit is to glorify God with 100 percent authentic faith.

Scott and Daron moved forward with boldness. Now it's your turn.

In the days ahead, ask God to help you formulate your life goals. Don't be afraid to dream. Submit all your hopes and desires to the Creator of dreams, and ask him to chart the right course for your life. Above all, ask the Lord for the strength to stay on course—the strength to be obedient to his ways.

▸ Read the following verses: "Not that I have already obtained all this, or have already been made perfect, but I press on to take hold of that for which Christ Jesus took hold of me. Brothers, I do not consider myself yet to have taken hold of it. But one thing I do: Forgetting what is behind and straining toward what is ahead, I press on toward the goal to win the prize for which God has called me heavenward in Christ Jesus" (Phil. 3:12–14).

How is the Christian life like a big race?

Name some things in life that cause Christians to stumble and veer off the path God has set before them.

What are some things that Christians need to do in order to stay spiritually strong?

▸ Read Psalm 139:23–24. This passage gives us insight about what it means to be honest with the Lord. (David and other psalmists wrote and spoke honestly about the full range of their responses to situations.)

Why do you think God wants us to be open and honest with him about all of our emotions, not just the pleasant ones?
How is being totally honest with God the first step toward discovering his will?

▸ Crack open a dictionary and read the definition of the word *commitment*.

What does it mean to be committed to God?
Does commitment mean perfection?

Truth Encounters

Wired to Win

Forgetting what is behind and straining toward what is ahead, I press on toward the goal to win the prize for which God has called me heavenward in Christ Jesus.

Philippians 3:13–14

Get Real

It's a sticky afternoon of baseball. At the bottom of the ninth inning, the scoreboard shows two outs. Waves of heat shimmer across a red-clay diamond. The pitcher's hands tremble as he eyes the next batter. Just one more out and his team takes the championship.

He winds up and delivers. With a resounding crack the batter makes contact, line driving the ball toward the mound. The pitcher lunges for it, but the ball slams into his wrist, fracturing both bones. Barely hesitating, he scoops up the ball, hurls it to first, and throws the runner out.

It's another victory from the mound, not to mention an amazing play. But here's what's most incredible: The pitcher isn't a pro or even in the minors. He's a teenager who delivers major-league moves despite having cerebral palsy—a major disability that often makes even walking a chore.

You just met Ron Padot of Jasper, Florida—a marvel on the mound, not to mention living proof of an awesome message: "Never say can't. If you have a goal, go for it. Believe in the abilities that God gave you and don't accept your limitations."

So exactly how does Ron handle cerebral palsy? And how was he able to develop the control and coordination necessary to play baseball? He says it all goes back to his love for sports (what else?!) and a talk that changed his life.

"I've always lived for sports, especially baseball. When I was seven, I desperately wanted to play T-ball. So Dad promised to work with me. First, he bought me a right-handed glove, and we tried to play catch. But I couldn't hang on to anything. My right hand just didn't have enough strength to grab the ball. I cried. I was so frustrated. I kept saying, 'I can't.' But Dad sat me down and said, 'Never say I can't. Always say I can, then find another way to accomplish the task.'

"Dad bought me a left-handed glove . . . and it worked. For the first time in my life, I caught a ball. Today, I'm still catching baseballs.

"I realized early in life that success would come from having buff brain cells, not muscles. Who knows? Maybe this handicap was a blessing in disguise. It has forced me to focus on my schoolwork and to never give up at anything I try. I always look for alternative ways of tackling other problems in life. I try never to let a problem get the best of me—just as my dad had said. Above all, God has given me the strength to accept life's challenges. He gives me the confidence to say, 'Yes, I can. I really can accomplish any goal I set my mind on.'"

So what's holding you back from reaching your goals? Fear? Procrastination? A shortage in the motivation department? Remember Ron's words: *I can.* Then tell yourself . . .

> *I can* because God broke the chains and set me free to live in wholeness, in fullness—because I've been given fullness in Christ.
> *I can* because God gives me the confidence to take risks, to fail, and to succeed.
> *I can* because God wired me to win.

Get Ready

> ‣ **John 15:16** In what ways does this verse give you confidence?
> ‣ **2 Corinthians 4:18** Why should you fix your eyes on what is unseen?
> ‣ **Colossians 3:15–17** Based on these verses, what is the key to success?

Get Going

> ‣ **Plot a course.** Divide a sheet of paper into two columns. On the left side write "My Goals." On the right side write "How I'm Going to Accomplish Them." The sky's the limit! Don't hold back—dream big! Jot down everything you want to do, or learn, or achieve. Now pray

over this list. Ask God to show you which goals are part of his plan—which ones you should pursue. Then ask him to show you how to achieve them. Over the next few weeks (or months), scratch off the goals that you think aren't part of God's will for your life and write down ideas on how you think God wants you to accomplish the remaining goals. Keep this sheet of paper in a handy place—like above your desk or in a prayer journal.

▸ **Memorize a promise.**

> Do you not know?
>> Have you not heard?
> The LORD is the everlasting God,
>> the Creator of the ends of the earth.
> He will not grow tired or weary,
>> and his understanding no one can fathom.
> He gives strength to the weary
>> and increases the power of the weak.
> Even youths grow tired and weary,
>> and young men stumble and fall;
> but those who hope in the LORD
>> will renew their strength.
> They will soar on wings like eagles;
>> they will run and not grow weary,
>> they will walk and not be faint.
>
> Isaiah 40:28–31

Day 23: God's Will (Part 1)

The Unknown Journey

> I will make you into a great nation
> and I will bless you;
> I will make your name great,
> and you will be a blessing.
>
> Genesis 12:2

Get Real

The journey ahead seems scary, yet Abram is obedient.

The Lord tells him, "Leave your country, your people, and your father's household and go to the land I will show you."

The seventy-five-year-old man and his family pull up their roots, step out of their comfort zone, and set off on a radical journey.

"I will make you into a great nation and I will bless you," the Lord promises Abram. "I will make your name great, and you will be a blessing."

Abram embraces the unknown. He and his family travel through a hostile land, where there is famine and death. But Abram is patient and holds firm to his faith. God prospers Abram—and fulfills his promise.

A promise from heaven whispered into the heart of a human—and the divine journey begins. That's the way a life with God starts. A voice says, "Follow me." If the human is obedient to God's will, he or she gets up and follows.

God chose Abram, one lonely man, to be the foundation of a new humanity. God spoke, and Abram did what God said. He stepped into the unknown with nothing to guide him but a voice—and the hope he put in his Creator.

The words have been spoken to you. Are you listening? How will you answer? If you follow, you will find what Abram discovered: What he left behind was nothing compared to what lay ahead. You will walk on a path filled with the solid promises of God.

God promised Abram that the entire world would be blessed because of what he did. Your promise is that your life will take on greater meaning and purpose—a whole new purpose for living, a whole new power to live in the joy of sins forgiven and wounds healed, a whole new degree of strength for the moment and hope for tomorrow.

Get Ready

> ▸ **Joshua 23:1–16** Based on this passage, what is the key to knowing God's will?
> ▸ **Psalm 27:14** Why is waiting for the Lord an important part of discovering his will?
> ▸ **Isaiah 30:19–22** Whose voice must we listen to?

Get Going

▸ **When the Lord opens doors—be faithful.** That's what being a Christian is all about. You don't have to be perfect to make an impact—just obedient.

▸ **As you seek God's will, be prepared to wait.** It may take a period of patient waiting before God speaks to us about an issue—a hope, a dream, a goal. Why? Because he has forgotten, or because it's not that important to him? Absolutely not! It's because in the process of making us wait, he is preparing us for his answer, which we may have missed had he spoken immediately. The Lord will not tell us some things instantaneously. Sometimes we have to wait a season of time—at least until we are prepared to listen.

▸ **Listen patiently.** These times of waiting may draw out and stretch our faith. He has promised to speak to our hearts, so we can expect him to, but he is not compelled to tell us everything we want to know the moment we desire the information.

Day 24: God's Will (Part 2)

Which Track, God?

Commit to the LORD whatever you do,
and your plans will succeed.

Proverbs 16:3

Get Real

Faster. The coach's words scream through Jeremy White's head. *Faster on each turn. Seventy laps. No rest.*

He and the five other speed skaters look like a long train as they race around the 400-meter ice rink. Jeremy is tailing the lead skater for now, but on the next turn, he'll pull off and drop to the rear of the pack. Then it will be Jeremy's turn to pace as hard as he can, with the other guys following him.

Every muscle is surging with pain, and his heart is pounding so hard it hurts to breathe. *How'd I ever get nicknames like Colorado Flash or Jean-Claude Van Jeremy?*

"Go! Go! Go!" barks the coach, as Jeremy takes the lead.

Jeremy shrugs off the stinging razors tearing through his quadriceps and focuses on his goal: competing in the winter Olympic Games.

Building endurance and pushing his twenty-two-year-old body to its limit six to eight hours a day, six days a week, is the only way to get there. "But if I didn't believe it was God's will for my life," he tells other racers, "I wouldn't spend another second on the ice."

As this book goes to press, Jeremy still hasn't made it to the Olympics. But he hasn't put away his skates. "Speed skating in the Olympics is my dream," he says, "yet if I don't make it, I'll put it in the past and look forward to whatever else God has planned for me. I know that everything that happens to me has a purpose. God's purpose. And his purpose is always best."

Jeremy has anchored his life to the right goal: seeking God's will. And the discipline and commitment is paying off. Each day, his body grows stronger, his skills sharpen, and he's one step closer to fulfilling his dreams. His faith in God is deepening too. The more this athlete spends training his spiritual life—reading the Bible, praying, and seeking God's guidance—the more God reveals himself to Jeremy.

The fact is, God's will is revealed when we seek him. God has already mapped out our lives since birth. But it's entirely up to him when he decides to make his presence and power known directly to us. And once this happens, our lives are forever changed.

Get Ready

> ▸ **Romans 8:28–39** How can you be confident that God is for you—even when things aren't going your way?
> ▸ **Romans 12:1–8** How should you test and approve what God's will is?

▸ **Philippians 3:20–21** Since your citizenship is in heaven, how does this affect your earthly goals?

Get Going

▸ **Steer clear of distractions.** Especially the ones that'll take you down a nowhere track. You know the ones—a lust for money (instead of God's riches), an appetite for immoral sex (instead of the genuine love that Christ offers), a thirst for alcohol and drugs (instead of the joy of pleasing our Creator).

▸ **Get on an eternal track.** Just as an athlete gives his or her all to a sport, Christians need to give the same commitment to God. Once you put God first in your life and trust him with all your heart, he will show you his power—power that you never imagined. His will for you far surpasses any of your own dreams and goals.

▸ **Keep your balance.** Satan knows exactly the right buttons to push! He sees your weak points and goes after them. But he can't destroy you, that is, if you don't let him. No matter how bad life gets, no matter how much you sin, Jesus still loves you. But it hurts the Lord when you disobey him. Christ wept for your sin, and he yearns for you to come back to him. When you blow it, confess your sins to God and ask him to help you get your life on the right track again.

Day 25: Commitment

Burn the Ships

For the eyes of the LORD range throughout the earth to strengthen those whose hearts are fully committed to him.

2 Chronicles 16:9

Get Real

It's a grueling journey, and the fleet of eleven ships is battered almost beyond repair. Even harder hit are the nerves of the crew.

"Has our captain gone mad?!" yells a sailor.

"He'll end up getting us all killed," complains another.

"I say we turn around and go back!" insists a crewman.

Suddenly, fear erupts on the decks. "Go back! Go back! Go back! Let's go back to the life we once knew."

But Hernán Cortés won't budge. He has amassed his battalion of 508 soldiers and 100 sailors and has set out on an important mission for the king of Spain: explore the New World.

Cortés silences the crowd. "Gentlemen, we can't go back now. This is our destiny. We were made for this moment."

Then he reminds his men of the words he had printed on a banner: "Brothers and comrades, let us follow the sign of the Holy Cross in true faith, for under this sign we shall conquer."

It works. And soon the ships reach Mexico. Yet Cortés doesn't let out a sigh of relief. He knows other storms are just on the horizon. So he quickly goes to work, disciplining his army, welding it into a cohesive force.

Then the famous conquistador does something that will be retold again and again in the history books: He orders his men to burn the ships. By doing so, Cortés actually saves the lives of his crew. Since the ships are so weather-beaten from the journey, returning to Spain would be risky. And by that single action, Cortés commits himself and his entire force to survival through conquest. It also ensures that they will keep their eyes on the New World, not on the life they left behind.

As Christians, Jesus has called us to burn our ships too. Following him involves a lifetime commitment. We have come to a whole new world through our relationship with Christ—and there's no turning back. But nobody said it would be easy (not even Christ).

Do you sometimes have doubts about the Lord's power in your life? (Are you sometimes a chameleon for Christ— a member of God's secret service?) If so, it's time to "burn a ship or two."

Accepting Christ in your heart is the best thing you've ever done. So don't worry a lot about being ridiculed and rejected when you don't go along with the crowd. Don't tremble in your boots when hard times hit. Jesus won't leave you all alone. You've got to trust God and take some risks.

It's God's plan that we move toward the goal of becoming more like his Son, Jesus Christ. This is a big goal; that's why God gave us a lifetime to work on it. But it all begins by burning the ships and keeping your eyes on the New World, not on the life you left behind.

I know what you're thinking: *That sounds good, Michael, but how do I do it?*

Glad you asked!

Get Ready

> ‣ **Deuteronomy 31:8** Does this verse give you the courage to press on?
> ‣ **Luke 9:62** Why does Christ demand radical commitment?
> ‣ **Hebrews 6:19** What is this "anchor for the soul"?

Get Going

‣ **Follow the Compass.** Jesus knows there will be hardships and times when we wish we could go back to "safer" ground. Remember that he is there for you. He'll help you through the tough times. He won't sit idly by, hoping you'll have the strength to withstand. He wants to provide the inner muscle it takes to combat the outer pressure you feel.

You can call out God's name and talk to him directly! The fact is that the Almighty God, Creator of the universe, King of Kings, Knower of all things loves you more than you'll ever imagine. (He's your biggest fan.)

‣ **Stay on course.** The shallow Christian simply puts his Bible on a shelf, purchases a wardrobe of "Christian" T-shirts, and then chooses to *wear* a slogan rather than *live* a faith. His favorite book is *A Lazy Man's Path to Heaven*. And since this guy knows God is forgiving, he thinks his ticket is paid.

But Jesus wants you to be a person of depth. He doesn't want you to sell out for what's comfortable or go back to the old life you once knew. He's calling you to plug in to his power through prayer and Bible study . . . and set your sights on a greater world ahead.

Learning to become more like Christ means spending time with him. Only the depth of God's Word gives you the depth of spirit that you and others can draw from.

▶ **Drop anchor.** As a Christian, you are expected to be a defender. How? By living a life of conscience. Jesus wants you to recognize sin and have the courage to stand up and say, "Hey, that's just not right."

Remember, the teen years only last a few short years. The next time you're in a tight spot, ask yourself this question: Am I willing to throw away what's right and settle for stuff that's wrong (just to please the crowd)?

Day 26: Obedience

Fangs of Danger

My God sent his angel, and he shut the mouths of the lions. They have not hurt me, because I was found innocent in his sight.

Daniel 6:22

Get Real

Obedience to God. Radical, unwavering submission to the one, true King—even at the risk of losing popularity, prestige, position. Even in the deadly grip of a lion's fangs.

Daniel knows this degree of obedience, and despite the order not to pray, he stays committed to God. After all, he's seen the Master's hand move in amazing ways—especially the time when three fellow believers were thrown into a blazing furnace. The flames were so hot that King Nebuchadnezzar's soldiers died as they threw Shadrach, Meshach, and Abednego into the fire. Yet the men of God stepped out of the furnace unharmed. Not a single hair on their heads was singed!

"Praise be to the God of Shadrach, Meshach, and Abednego," Nebuchadnezzar proclaimed. "They trusted in him and defied the king's command and were willing to give up their lives rather than serve or worship any god except their own God."

But will the hard-hearted people of the world ever learn? Now, many years later, the opposition to God and his people continues. This time, Babylon's administrators have convinced the new king, Darius the Mede, to issue an unjust decree: "Anyone who prays to any god or man during the next thirty days, except to you, O king, shall be thrown into the lions' den."

Daniel doesn't flinch. He kneels at his upstairs window—the one opened toward Jerusalem—and prays three times a day, giving thanks to God . . . just as always.

"Did you not publish a decree?" the administrators ask the king.

"The decree stands," the ruler replies, and Daniel is quickly thrown into the lions' den.

"May your God, whom you serve continually, rescue you," the king tells Daniel. Then a stone is placed over the mouth of the den.

Will Daniel's life end with the fierce swipe of a lion's paw? Not a chance! Just as with the miracle in the furnace, God protects and prospers his obedient child.

Daniel emerges unscratched, and King Darius is overjoyed: "For he is the living God and he endures forever. . . . He rescues and he saves; he performs signs and wonders in the heavens and on the earth. He has rescued Daniel from the power of the lions" (Dan. 6:26–27).

Radical obedience. Unwavering submission to the King of Kings. That's how Daniel lived his faith. He didn't know exactly what would happen to him in the pit of the lions' den, but he did know this: God is God, the one and only God, and he can be trusted—even when a dozen lions are poised to pounce.

Hopefully you'll never have to prove your faith in the face of hungry beasts or the belly of a fiery furnace. But like it or not, you encounter choices every day that test your beliefs: the temptation to lie (or just bend the truth a bit), a struggle with lust, curiosity about drugs and alcohol. How do you choose? Do your decisions honor God and speak boldly of your obedience to him?

Get Ready

> ▸ **Daniel 1:1–21** What are the rewards of obedience to God?
> ▸ **Matthew 9:9–13** Do you desire Matthew's level of obedience?
> ▸ **Hebrews 10:35–39** How can you keep from being one who "shrinks back"?

Get Going

▸ **Count the cost.** Living for Christ is expensive. It costs everything—especially stuff like trust, commitment, and 100-percent, rock-solid obedience to him. The choice is yours. Will you follow the crowd and conform to the world, or, like Daniel, commit yourself to standing strong for God (and maybe even leading your friends in a radical eternal direction)? It all starts with the first step: a desire to follow Christ.

▸ **Remove the roadblocks.** This is the next crucial step. Ask Jesus to search your heart and to help you pinpoint specific sins that are holding you back from an obedient relationship with him. After praying, take out a notebook and a pen. On the top of one page write "Things I Must Get Right with God." Then list all the stuff you need to confess to the Lord. Ask God to do a deep work in your soul. Allow him to examine every area of your life. (Example: Perhaps you have a problem with envy or a bad temper. Confess these sins to God.)

▸ **Do business with the Lord without delay.** Commit yourself to be obedient to him in *every* area of your life. While the cost is expensive, the reward is unreal: "This is the confidence we have in approaching God: that if we ask anything according to his will, he hears us. And if we know that he hears us—whatever we ask—we know that we have what we asked of him" (1 John 5:14–15).

Day 27: Spirit-Filled Living

A Leap of Faith

I will not leave you as orphans; I will come to you.

John 14:18

Get Real

As I stand at the bottom of a three-story tower and look up, I can't help gasping.

"So you want me to climb to the top—then jump off?!" I say to my friend, who just happens to be a professional stuntman. "You've got to be nuts!"

Eddie Matthews pats my back. "Piece of cake," he says with a grin. "Stuntmen practically do this in their sleep! As long as you listen to my voice and follow my instruction, you'll hit the mark." (Meaning I'd land safely on an air bag.)

I'm in Southern California on assignment for *Breakaway* magazine. My mission: Learn what it's like to be a stuntman by . . . get this . . . *becoming a stuntman for a day!* (Okay, I'm not actually going to act in a movie, but I will get a taste of some of the stuff fall guys do.)

I'm at a "stuntman ranch" just north of Los Angeles and a stone's throw from several movie studio backlots. It's a place where some of Hollywood's best come to sharpen their skills and learn new techniques.

As I muster up my courage and slowly make my way up the tower, the ladder begins to wobble.

"Don't worry," Eddie yells up to me. "A recent earthquake loosened a few things."

Earthquake? Yikes!

My heart kicks into high gear as I reach the top and look down. "I'm supposed to hit that tiny red mark on the air bag?" I mumble. "Impossible!"

Suddenly, panic. Adrenaline surges through my veins and every muscle seems to tremble. Even worse, my internal "idiot alert" is beeping way out of control: *Warning: Stress overload. Fear of heights now at full capacity. Ego meltdown imminent.*

"On the count of three—jump!" Eddie yells. "Don't forget what I told you. Listen to my voice and follow my instruction. You'll be okay."

Instruction?! Oh, yeah. I try to push back my fear and concentrate on the techniques Eddie taught me, but a vision of my mom flashes before my eyes. With her nostrils flaring and her hands on her hips, she recites every lecture from my childhood about *not* jumping off high places (including three-story towers).

"O-N-E . . ."

Breathing becomes an extreme chore, and that spicy Gordita I ate at Taco Bell last month revisits my stomach. (What exactly is in a Gordita anyway?!)

"T-W-O . . ."

Another distraction. This time it's from my photographer. "Don't jump, Mike. This is a bad idea! I want you around for future photo shoots."

"T-H-R-E-E!"

Eddie's advice swirls through my brain: "Listen to my voice. Follow my instruction." I swallow, then take a step . . .

Sorry, Mom, but—

"Y-E-E-O-O-W-E-E!"

A half second later I'm lying on my back with a yellow nylon air bag hugging me. I open my eyes and see Eddie's smile. "Welcome back to earth, Mr. Fall Guy!"

I glance back up at the tower. "Can I go again?"

After a dozen high falls, I had gotten more than a taste of what stuntmen do. But I never expected that taking a leap of faith would teach me a lesson about life—and trusting the Holy Spirit for direction.

Whatever major life decision you're facing—which school to attend, whom to marry, what career path to follow—you can trust the Holy Spirit for guidance.

The third Person of the Trinity—the Holy Spirit—is our Guide, Helper, Strengthener, and Advocate, sent by Christ to live in us and to control every aspect of our lives. Like the Father and the Son, God the Holy Spirit is to be believed and obeyed.

Get Ready

▸ **Joel 2:28–32** Who receives the Holy Spirit?
▸ **John 14:25–27** Who is the Counselor?
▸ **Acts 2:1–21** How does the Holy Spirit guide each of us?

Get Going

▸ **Guided by the Holy Spirit.** He is "another Counselor" who lives in us and with us and around us. Can you sense his presence in your life? Can you hear his voice directing your steps? You can "hit the mark" and experience all the goals and plans God has for you. Call out to the Holy Spirit for guidance and follow the instruction God has given us through the Scriptures.

▸ **Encouraged by the Holy Spirit.** He will take away your fears—your fear of rejection, your fear of change, your fear of failure—and give you the hope and courage you need to face any challenge life throws your way. Remember, it was Christ who said, "You will receive power when the Holy Spirit comes on you; and you will be my witnesses" (Acts 1:8).

▸ **Comforted by the Holy Spirit.** In times of trouble—especially those moments when everything and everyone seems too weird to handle—the Holy Spirit comes and carries you toward wholeness and peace. Trust him.

Day 28: True Fulfillment

Crossroads of Life

The LORD is near to all who call on him,
to all who call on him in truth.
He fulfills the desires of those who fear him;
he hears their cry and saves them.

Psalm 145:18–19

Get Real

It's May 1990, and Saddam Hussein is making threats again. This time the Iraqi leader is vowing to crush his tiny southern neighbor, Kuwait, then point his missiles west and wipe out Israel with nerve gas.

As CBS reporter Dave Dolan follows the Middle East saga, he can't help but wonder the obvious: *Why is the world tolerating this madman?*

Dave gets a clue at a standing-room-only press conference in Jerusalem. He and other journalists from every major news outlet on the planet aim their microphones and cameras at a delegation of American politicians. A White House representative steps forward and clears his throat. The room grows silent.

"The United States will continue to do business with Saddam Hussein," the man says. "The president is hopeful that Mr. Hussein will cease from making threats against Israel. . . ."

Dave squeezes his eyes shut and swallows hard, trying not to give away the bitterness welling up inside. *Ludicrous*, he tells himself. *Saddam Hussein is an evil man . . . and the United States wants business as usual?!*

"Oil" isn't the answer Dave is willing to accept. As far as this journalist is concerned, Saddam must be held accountable for his atrocities against the people of the Middle East.

After a few more official remarks from the White House, the floor is opened for questions. A flurry of hands go up, and Dave is called upon.

"Saddam is known as the 'Butcher of Baghdad' here in the Middle East," Dave says. "He has used nerve gas on his own people, the Kurds, and has killed several members of his own family. Now he's threatening to wipe out half of Israel with nerve gas, and the White House wants business as usual? Shouldn't we stop doing business with Saddam and put him in his place?"

The American politicians, seemingly embarrassed by the question, shrug their shoulders and move on to other questions. Dave shakes his head, completely distraught.

Lord God, I fear what will happen, the veteran journalist prays to himself. *Let the world leaders look beyond "business" and see the evil they're up against.*

Three months later, on August 2, Dave isn't surprised when Iraq invades Kuwait. He's not even stunned by the events that follow: On January 17, 1991, a U.S.-led coalition retaliates with Operation Desert Storm, launching the Gulf War.

Facing down political leaders, traveling throughout one of the world's most dangerous places . . . uncovering what's behind the headlines. It's all in a day's work for

Dave. Yet this veteran journalist does more than just report the news. He says he's on a mission from God.

"When I was a young man, the Lord placed in me a desire for missionary radio work, as well as a heart for Israel," Dave says. "Never in my wildest dreams did I imagine that the two would one day meet."

In addition to his work with CBS, Dave serves as a broadcast journalist for Transworld Radio's Voice of Hope network and is committed to transmitting the gospel throughout the Holy Land.

Dave has spent much of his life living and working in a place that's often described as the "crossroads of life"— Jerusalem. He has walked in the footsteps of Jesus and has looked upon a chaotic culture that's continually torn apart by political and religious disagreements, a culture that often values man's rules over God's. "A people," Dave says, "that represents all of humanity."

But as this journalist walks among Israel's many ancient sights, he is reminded of an awesome truth: While the glory of this world is fleeting and flawed by strife, true fulfillment can be found by knowing intimately, loving intensely, serving passionately, and trusting completely Jesus Christ. Eternal peace is at the core of God's gift of salvation.

"Just as it's written in the Book of Acts, Jesus will return to the Holy Land—the same place where he went up into heaven," Dave says. "A restored Israel is very close to the heart of God. It's not only the restoration of a people to a land—but all people to their God. This is where true fulfillment can be found. This is what we all should be seeking."

Get Ready

▸ **Matthew 7:24–27** What do these verses tell you about faith in God?

▸ **John 6:25–33** What is the "food" Christ offers?

▸ **Romans 8:18–25** Why do you think a life committed to God is far more fulfilling than a worldly existence?

Get Going

▸ **Don't look to the world for true fulfillment— look to God.** It's kind of ironic that the "Holy Land" is one of the most chaotic regions of the world. But in the words of Dave Dolan, "Strong forces, based on ancient religious beliefs, are at work in the Arab-Israeli struggle." Yet there is hope even today for the troubled Middle East, as well as the entire world. Every one of Abraham's children—Arab, Jew, and Gentile alike—has the same opportunity of receiving God's gift of eternal life, offered in his chosen Messiah.

▸ **Love Christ first.** Scripture reminds us to focus on the Lord and to recognize that Christians have the key to a significant, marvelous, joyful, and fulfilling life. It's all grounded on a relationship with Jesus Christ. Get to know the voice of the Lord as clearly as you are able. Strengthen your relationship with him *first*, then devote your energy to the other relationships in your life.

Salt and Light

Extreme Faith for Extreme Times

Beth is frustrated. She can't seem to find the right words to explain why the school ski trip is off-limits. What's more, the timing can't be worse. Tina is just now becoming a close friend, and Beth doesn't want to ruin their friendship.

"Look, Tina," Beth says, her eyes darting around the room, "I just can't go . . . okay?! I'm not being stuck up, I just have other stuff to do."

Beth knows the weekend getaway will be a guy-chasing, drinking bash, which goes against her values. Besides, her parents would never let her go on an unsupervised trip.

Why is Clint's heart pounding? He's hanging out at Burger King with three friends. Suddenly, the subject changes to religion.

"Religion is for losers," says one of the guys. "And the Bible is full of fairy tales."

"I know what you mean," says another. "Most Christians are narrow-minded hypocrites anyway. Who needs all that religion junk?"

Clint, who just happens to be serious about his relationship with Christ, keeps his mouth shut. But as he leaves the restaurant, he carries with him a lot of unidentified emotions—not to mention a bunch of guilt.

Kellie scrunches into a tiny ball and rests her chin on her knee. The conversation between her history study partners is almost too much to handle.

"Are you sure, Holly?" Danielle presses. "I mean, you could be a little late because of midterms, stress—stuff like that."

"Look, I'm not just a *little* late. Trust me, I know what's happening inside my own body." Holly puts her hand on her stomach and looks down. "I'm about fourteen weeks along."

"Have you told your parents?" Melanie asks.

"Are you kidding?! They'd freak."

"How about . . . him?" Danielle adds.

Holly shakes her head. "No."

A stabbing pain shoots through Kellie's stomach as she listens. As a Christian, she just can't imagine facing such a difficult dilemma. And what should she say?

Beth, Clint, and Kellie feel as though they're between a rock and a hard place. After all, it's not easy to stand up for what you believe when you feel outnumbered. Yet keeping your mouth shut or alienating yourself from the world isn't the answer either.

While there isn't a simple formula for sharing your beliefs, it all boils down to this: If you identify yourself with Christ, and if you're confident about what you believe and where you're headed as a Christian, it will be much more natural to live your faith around non-Christian friends. In other words, confidence is the key. If you're not uptight about being a Christian, your friends won't be bothered by it either.

Now, as far as what to say to your non-Christian friends, let's look at some right and wrong approaches.

One approach: Develop a holier-than-thou attitude. Alienating the world by preaching a bunch of "dos" and "don'ts" or by speaking in Christianese—a language most nonbelieving earthlings don't understand—isn't exactly what Christ has in mind for your life. Neither is living your faith within the safety of your church or a tight circle of like-minded friends. God wants us to be salt and light to the sick, not a pungent medicine that nobody can swallow. Jesus himself was often criticized for hanging around with the "wrong" kind of people. His response: "It is not the healthy who need a doctor, but the sick" (Matt. 9:12).

A better approach: Step out with confidence. The world desperately needs to see a solid Christian example. But if Christianity is lived only within the safety of church walls and tight circles of like-minded friends, how can we make an impact? How can God use us in the lives of those who are blind to the truth?

It would be cool for Beth or Kellie to be honest and say something like this: "I'm not into drinking or the party scene, that's why I'm not going. But I still value our friendship. I'm a Christian, so I believe . . ." or "I can't imagine all the stress you're going through with a pregnancy, but I know things are going to be okay."

One approach: Keep quiet and blend in. Too many Christian teens choose this approach. They want to be members of God's secret service, so their speech and actions are no different from those of non-Christians. And when God becomes the topic of conversation, they clam up. But the Bible instructs us not to blend in with the world (see John 17:14–16).

A better approach: Speak up with confidence. People respect someone who is committed to what he or she believes, someone who isn't wishy-washy. Unlike keeping quiet or alienating yourself, this approach offers Christians the most honest and challenging lifestyle.

It would be cool for Clint to be direct and say something like this: "Christians aren't perfect, but they're not all hypocrites. Hey, I'm a Christian, and I believe what the Bible teaches. Here's why."

Check Your Pulse

▸ When the pressure hits, do you catch yourself hiding your faith or speaking up (even at the risk of being unpopular)?

▸ How can you develop the courage of Daniel?

▸ Do you have an eternal perspective? (In other words, do you care more about pleasing God or pleasing the world?)

CONCLUSION

Iron-Willed Christians

Congratulations! You've reached the end of this book. You've covered a lot of ground during the past few weeks.

▸ You now have a deeper understanding of your faith, not to mention a better handle on why the Good News is actually the greatest news of all!

▸ You're plugged in to the truth. You know what the Messiah did nearly two thousand years ago—he came into the world, died on a cross, then was resurrected and went to heaven. You know what that means for all who commit their lives to him—salvation (eternal life), liberation (freedom from sin), and restoration (healing of the brokenhearted).

▸ As a committed Christian, your life is being radically transformed by this truth. You are someone who can't possibly sit still and stay quiet.

▶ You've accepted the mission of living your faith and telling the world what it is that anchors your life. You've made the commitment to get real, get ready, and get going.

But before we go our separate ways, let me remind you of two important facts about your faith: (1) walking the Christian walk is often hard, yet (2) you can make it if you choose to trust Jesus and step out with an iron-willed commitment.

What's an iron-willed commitment? Read all of Hebrews 11, then focus on the following verses:

> Let us throw off everything that hinders and the sin that so easily entangles, and let us run with perseverance the race marked out for us. Let us fix our eyes on Jesus, the author and perfecter of our faith, who for the joy set before him endured the cross, scorning its shame, and sat down at the right hand of the throne of God. Consider him who endured such opposition from sinful men, so that you will not grow weary and lose heart.

> Hebrews 12:1–3

Jesus overcame death on the cross so that—through his power—each one of us can overcome the obstacles that stand in our way . . . no matter how hopeless the situation may seem.

It's this realization that has made a difference in my own walk with Jesus. Through the years, I've discovered that I'm not alone in my struggles. I've learned that every Christian, at one time or another, wrestles with various hurts and fears, even feelings of inadequacy. The truth is, as a Christian—as a young man or woman who is head-ing down the road to eternal life—life is more often difficult than easy.

Pressing on with an iron will is the key. That's what Jesus did as he went to the cross. And he overcame death and the struggles of this world just for you and me. He headed down a road that took him to his physical death, but he also walked down a spiritual road that led to life.

He wants to take you down that life-giving road too.

Michael Ross is editor of Focus on the Family's *Breakaway* magazine and a featured speaker at the national Life on the Edge events. He is an award-winning writer, as well as a columnist for *Living with Teenagers* magazine. In addition, he has authored and coauthored several books, including *Faith Encounters* and a science fiction series for young readers titled Space Station Chronicles. Michael and his wife, Tiffany, live in Colorado Springs.